THE WELL DRESSED POTATO

Christie Katona
Thomas Katona

BRISTOL PUBLISHING ENTERPRISES, INC.
San Leandro, California

A Nitty Gritty® Cookbook

Printed in the United States of America.

ISBN 1-55867-092-0

Cover design: Frank Paredes
Front cover photography: John Benson
Food stylist: Suzanne Carreiro
Illustrator: James Balkovek

CONTENTS

ALL ABOUT POTATOES

Potatoes have held a reputation for a long time as a starchy and fattening food, and have long been considered a side dish or accompaniment to the main course. Finally, this unfair reputation has been stripped away. Nutritionists have shown that potatoes are low in calories, are an excellent source of complex carbohydrates, are high in vitamins and fiber, and contain no fat or cholesterol. An average baked potato (sans toppings) has about 110 calories or about the same number of calories as a large apple or ½ cup of cottage cheese.

We view the potato as a wholesome base like rice to which you can add an endless variety of delicious toppings and sauces that can be either extraordinarily rich or as healthy and diet conscious as you like; the choice is yours. In any case, the potato can be a meal in itself, as the recipes in this book will show you.

We have included a wide variety of recipes to suite almost every palate. You will find international recipes from Europe, the Middle East, Asia, Mexico and the Caribbean. There are seafood dishes like *Scampi Marnier* and elegant poultry and meat dishes like *Chicken Boursin*, *Veal Picatta* and *Pork Marsala*. We have included low-calorie dishes, vegetarian dishes, and delicious dishes that use sweet potatoes and yams. There is also a section on fast family meals for busy parents.

In addition to the recipes, included is some interesting background information on potatoes and basic information you should have for buying, storing, preparing, and serving your potato dishes.

We sincerely hope you will enjoy preparing and serving these dishes as much as we did. Bon Appetit!

SOUTH AMERICAN ORIGINS

The potato originated in the Peruvian Andes of South America and was one of the major staples in the diet of the Incas. Some experts estimate that the Incas of Peru were cultivating potatoes as early as 500 B.C., although the potatoes they cultivated were smaller and more irregular than the genetically superior potatoes we have in our grocery stores. Spanish explorers were the first to discover potatoes in the Andean village of Sorocota in 1537 and subsequently introduced them to Spain, where they were cultivated as a food crop. Dutch explorers also introduced them to Southeast Asia at about the same time. From Spain, cultivation of potatoes spread slowly to continental Europe and then to England; however, England did not cultivate them as a crop until the mid-18th century.

Since the potato grows well in cool, moist areas, it flourished in England and Ireland and became a major food staple in those countries. Many people remember the Irish Potato Famine from their history lessons. When the potato crops failed between 1845 and 1847 due to a blight, nearly one million people starved to death in Ireland and about the same number emigrated to escape the famine.

The first potatoes in the United States arrived at Jamestown, Virginia in 1621 but were not planted as a crop until a group of Scotch-Irish Presbyterian immigrants planted them near Londenderry, New Hampshire in 1719. Today, potatoes are grown in many states, with the top five potato-producing states being Idaho, Washington, North Dakota, Colorado and Wisconsin in that order.

Potatoes are the fourth largest commercial crop in the world. In the U.S., the per capita consumption of potatoes has steadily increased, and reached an all time high of 131 pounds in 1991 or about 390 potatoes per person per year. Of that, about 36 percent were fresh and the remaining were processed in some manner. By far, frozen potatoes (french fries) made up the bulk of the processed foods, followed by potato chips, and then dehydrated potato flakes. In 1991, about 5 billion pounds of french fries were produced in the United States. The potato industry estimates that one in every three meals consumed in the United States contains some form of potatoes.

POTATO VARIETIES

The potatoes we are used to in the grocery stores are actually edible tubers that are a member of the Nightshade family of plants. The potato portion grows underground at the end of the plant stems, while above ground, the plant stem and dark green leaves somewhat resemble the leaves and stocks of a tomato plant. Potato plants develop small green fruits at times which, like Nightshade, are poisonous. The "eyes" which develop on potatoes are the means by which potatoes generate new plants. It is those eyes, or buds, which are planted to start a new crop rather than the poisonous fruit which develops on the leaves.

Sweet potatoes and yams are traditional holiday fare in the United States. Sweet potatoes are a member of the Morning Glory family rather than the Nightshade family. They were also discovered by European explorers in South America and were a staple in the Aztec diet. Yams resemble sweet potatoes, but are not even remotely related via their plant families. We have included a good number of recipes for these tasty tubers ranging from soups to desserts.

The potatoes we use for baking, boiling and frying come in many shapes and sizes but are generally classified by producers into categories by shape and skin color. From the producers' point of view, potatoes are primarily classified as round or long, and then as white, red or russet. From the consumers' point of view, potatoes are either thin-skinned, which are best suited for boiling, or thick-skinned, which are best suited for baking and frying. The most common thin-skinned varieties are the short round reds, the round whites, and the long whites. The thin-skinned varieties are sometimes referred to as "new potatoes," since they usually come fresh from the fields without having spent time in storage. This is partly due to the fact that the thin-skinned varieties do not store as well as the thick-skinned varieties.

The most common thick-skinned variety is the Russet Burbank, named after Luther Burbank who developed the variety in the early 1870s. It is also commonly known as the "Idaho potato," although this variety is also grown Washington, Oregon and other potato-producing states.

The Russet Burbank is the most commonly used potato for baking as well as for commercial processing. Processors desire a potato that has a high specific gravity and that is low in sugar. Specific gravity is a measure of the solid versus water content of the potato. A potato that has a high solid content will require less dehydration during processing, will absorb less oil if deep-fried, and generally produces a lighter and fluffier baked potato.

Here are the most common varieties of potatoes grown in the United States:

Russet

Burbank	(most preferred for baking and commercial processing)
Centennial	(has a pleasing appearance, but is too high in water content to be a good baker)
Lemhi	
Norgold	(next preferred baked after the Burbank)
Norkotah	(fairly new variety with qualities similar to the Centennial)

Round White

Chippewa	Norchip
Irish Cobbler	Ontario
Kennebec (favored by many potato	Sebago
chip producers)	Shepody
Katahdin	Superior
Monona	

Round Red (firm texture and thin skin)

LaRouge	Red McClure
Norland	Red Pontiac
Red La Soda	

Long White

White Rose   (thin skin and firm waxy texture; holds shape well when cooked)

NUTRITION

Potatoes have been maligned in the past as a starchy, high caloric food when in actuality, a potato has about the same calories as a large apple and it is high in nutritional value. Potatoes are an excellent source of complex carbohydrates. They are high in vitamins, high in fiber, and contain no fat or cholesterol. Of course, if you slather a potato with butter, sour cream, bacon and other high fat foods, all bets are off.

The complex carbohydrates provided by potatoes are digested more slowly than simple carbohydrates like sugar. As a result, they provide a sustained and steady amount of energy over a longer period of time, so you will be able to go longer between meals without feeling hungry.

The following tables provide the nutritional rating for 1 medium U.S. potato (150 grams or 5.33 oz.). However, these can vary depending on the potato type and where it is grown.

U.S. Recommended Daily Allowance

Protein	6%	Vitamin B6	15%
Vitamin A	*	Folic Acid	8%
Vitamin C	50%	Phosphorus	8%
Thiamin (B1)	8%	Magnesium	8%
Riboflavin (B2)	2%	Zinc	2%
Niacin	10%	Copper	8%
Calcium	*	Pantothenic Acid	4%
Iron	6%		

*Contains less than 2% of the USRDA for this nutrient.

Nutrient

Protein	3 g	Potassium	750 mg
Carbohydrate	23 g	Dietary Fiber	2.7 g
Fat	0 g	Calories	110
Sodium	10 mg	Cholesterol	0 mg

Most of the minerals in a potato are found in the cambian, which is the narrow layer just below the outer skin, whereas the other nutritional elements are found throughout the potato. So if you want your minerals, eat those skins.

TIPS ABOUT HEALTHY TOPPINGS

While this book is not dedicated to low-cal recipes, we have segregated a group of recipes into a section of this book for those interested in watching their waistlines (page 76). These recipes use ingredients which are low in fat and cholesterol content but are still delicious. If you experiment yourself, we suggest the following toppings which are healthy, nutritious, and generally low in calories for average quantities:

plain yogurt
low fat cottage cheese
low cal creamy dressings
fresh mushrooms
green onions
shredded carrots
cauliflower
broccoli

green peppers
diced tomatoes
sprouts
chives
sunflower seeds
sesame seeds
green beans

HOW TO SELECT POTATOES

Select potatoes that are firm, clean, smooth to the touch and regular in shape. Although shape does not affect the taste, you will appreciate how much easier they are to peel. In general, potatoes with fewer eyes and that have shallow eyes are higher in quality.

Avoid potatoes that are cracked, have sprouts, are wilted or wrinkled, or that have a green appearance or soft dark areas.

Note: Occasionally you may have come across potatoes that have dark areas within when cut in cross-section. These dark areas are caused by frostbite. Unfortunately, you cannot detect this damage by examining the outside of the potato.

STORAGE

Store potatoes in a cool, dark, well-ventilated area. Too much light causes potatoes to turn green, to taste bitter and to sprout. Most potato experts agree that the ideal storage temperature is between 45°F and 48°F. Warmer temperatures tend to cause sprouting and/or wrinkling. Cooler temperatures tend to break down the starches within and the potatoes will develop a sweet taste. This breakdown of the starches also causes the potatoes to darken in color when fried. For that reason, do not store potatoes in the refrigerator. Also, avoid storing them in plastic bags since potatoes deteriorate more quickly in plastic than in burlap or cardboard boxes.

PREPARATION
Washing

If you will be baking the potato, scrub it in cold water with a vegetable brush and remove any sprouts without breaking the skin. Some restaurants which serve large volumes of potatoes actually put the potatoes in dish racks and send them through the dishwasher (without the soap of course). If you will be peeling the potatoes, using a potato peeler or a thin paring knife. This is where you will appreciate buying smooth and regularly shaped potatoes. If you will be peeling large quantities of potatoes, you may want to submerge the peeled potatoes under water to preserve the whiteness until you are ready to cook them. However, also be aware that soaking them for long periods of time can leach the vitamins out and cause the potatoes to absorb too much water.

Cooking

Conventional oven: Place the washed and dried potatoes on a baking sheet or a "spud rack." If you are unfamiliar with a spud rack, it consists of 4 to 6 thin, vertical metal tines which are attached to a handle and allow you to impale the potatoes in an upright position. The metal tines help transfer the heat into the potato while also providing a steam vent which aids in producing the flakiness desired in a good baked potato. If you don't use a spud rack, make sure each potato is pierced at least once with a fork.

If you like to eat the potato skins as we do, and are not concerned with calories, you may wish to grease the outside skin with oil, butter, or margarine at this point to keep the skins soft. Do not place potatoes in foil since this steams them and causes too much moisture to be retained.

Baking time depends on the size. As a rough guide, bake at 425°F for 40 minutes for small potatoes, 50 minutes for medium size potatoes, and 60 minutes for large potatoes. If you want to be sure, use a thermometer. The potatoes are done when the internal temperature reads between 210°F and 220°F on the thermometer.

Convection oven: Preparation for convection cooking is identical to that for the conventional oven except that the cooking time and/or temperature is lowered, since the forced air circulation transfers the heat to the potatoes more quickly than the conventional oven. When placing the potatoes on the racks, make sure there is sufficient clearance between the potatoes for air circulation. As a guide, cook at 375°F for 30 to 45 minutes depending on size. Again, if you want to be sure, use an instant-reading thermometer to check for doneness.

Microwave oven: Generally, potatoes will cook far more quickly in a microwave; however, potatoes cooked this way tend to have wetter interiors and softer skins than those cooked in conventional or convection ovens. Try to use potatoes of uniform size so that all potatoes will have the same cooking time.

Wash but do not dry the potatoes and then pierce each potato once through the skin at the center. To help control the moisture content, wrap each potato in a microwave-safe paper towel.

If cooking more than 2, arrange the potatoes in a circle like a set of spokes on a wheel.

Cook on high for 4 to 5 minutes for a single large potato. As a general guideline, add 3 minutes for each additional potato. Note that it is somewhat difficult to estimate microwave cooking times since there is quite a variation in the wattage between various models of microwave ovens.

Most microwave ovens also have a rotating plate to promote even cooking. If yours does not, rearrange the potatoes about half way through the cooking and then continue until done.

The potatoes are done when they feel soft when squeezed with an oven mitt or when the internal temperature reads between 210°F and 220°F on a thermometer. Remember, if you cook different size potatoes at the same time, the smaller ones will be done sooner.

Let the potatoes rest in a paper towel for 2 minutes after removing them from the microwave before serving.

Electric potato baker: A new kitchen appliance on the market allows you to bake 2 potatoes in about 25 minutes. Two metal skewers inserted into the potatoes speed cooking time, and the device uses only ⅛ the power of a conventional oven.

SERVING

For the majority of the recipes in this book, you will be using baked russet potatoes. The best method for serving them attractively is a method called "blossoming." Using a fork, pierce the skin in the shape of a cross in the middle of the potato. Then, press the ends towards the center, which causes the meat of the potato to blossom upward. Alternately, you can split the potato horizontally down its length, and then use the fork to manually fluff the potato meat. For the best appearance, avoid cutting with a knife since this tends to flatten the surface.

ABOUT OUR RECIPES

When we first started thinking about this book it seemed like an overwhelming task to come up with dozens of different potato toppings. Now, the problem is knowing when to stop. As a busy married couple, with children(!), we believe cooking should be fun, and food should be delicious, nutritious and easy to fix. It's frustrating to spend a lot of time, money, effort and energy on food and then have the recipe turn out to be something the dog turns its nose up at. We think a recipe is just a good place to start - what you do in the privacy of your own kitchen is your business. If you need to substitute ingredients or your children refuse to eat artichokes, feel free to use what's on hand.

Here are some things to consider when you prepare a recipe for the first time:

- Read all the way through the recipe before you begin.
- Get all of the equipment out and ready.
- Make sure you have the ingredients and utensils on hand.
- Bring the butter, eggs, etc. to room temperature.
- Do all of the grating, chopping, defrosting and opening before you start.

- Preheat the oven, if necessary.

- Measure carefully.

- Use the temperatures given for baking but test for doneness about two-thirds of the way through the allotted time. Increase or decrease the time as necessary.

- Make sure you have adequate storage room in the refrigerator if required.

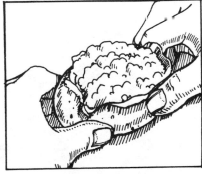

SAUCES AND POTATO BAR

CLASSIC WHITE SAUCE

Makes: 2 cups

Sauces can be fun and infinitely versatile once you master the basic technique. It's important to use a heavy-bottomed pan, and stir with either a wooden spoon or whisk. The butter and flour mixture is the thickening agent, called a "roux." Heating the liquid before adding it to the roux helps the sauce go together more evenly. It's important to stir in one direction only and stir constantly!

¼ cup butter
¼ cup flour

2 cups warm milk
salt and white pepper to taste

In a heavy-bottomed saucepan over medium heat, melt butter. Sprinkle with flour and stir constantly so roux bubbles but does not brown. Gradually add warm milk to mixture, stirring constantly until a smooth sauce forms. Season to taste.

VARIATIONS

- **Veloute Sauce:** Use chicken stock instead of milk.
- **Supreme Sauce:** Use chicken stock instead of milk. Beat 2 egg yolks with 2 tbs. heavy cream and blend into sauce without boiling.
- **Mornay Sauce:** Stir 1 cup shredded cheese into *Classic White Sauce*.

DEMI-GLACE

When Christie studied cooking at the Cordon Bleu in London she learned how to make all the wonderful classic French sauces from scratch. If you enjoy cooking and want to experiment, this is a quick Demi-Glace which you can make in quantity and freeze.

3 tbs. oil
1 carrot
1 small onion
1 stalk celery
3 tbs. flour
2 cups brown bone stock

a few mushroom peelings
1 tsp. tomato puree
a bouquet garni: 1 bay leaf, a sprig of
   thyme and 2 parsley stalks in a spice
   bag or cheesecloth
salt and pepper to taste

With a food processor or by hand, finely chop carrot, onion and celery. Heat oil in a shallow saucepan and add vegetables. Cook over low heat until vegetables are barely colored and softened. Stir in flour and continue to cook slowly, stirring with a metal spoon until a good russet brown. Draw vegetables aside in pan and add 1½ cups of stock and remaining ingredients. Bring to a boil and half cover with a lid. Simmer for 25 minutes. At this point, add reserved ½ cup of cold stock and tip the pan so fat can be skimmed off. Strain sauce through a sieve. Taste and season lightly. Can be frozen.

PARMESAN SAUCE

Makes 1½ cups

For a quick vegetarian topping, steam or microwave vegetables of your choice and spoon into a baked potato. Top with this wonderful sauce. It's particularly good with broccoli, carrots and cauliflower.

½ cup mayonnaise
½ cup whipping cream
½ cup sour cream
¼ cup grated Parmesan cheese
2 tsp. fresh lemon juice

Combine all ingredients in a saucepan and whisk over low heat until smooth and cheese is melted. Be careful not to boil.

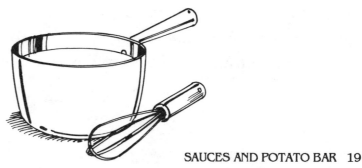

SAUCE IDEAS

Almost any leftover meat, seafood or vegetables can be added to a basic sauce and served over a baked potato for a quick and economical entrée. Let your imagination create endless combinations. Here are some ideas to get you started.

BASIC RECIPE

2 cups sauce
2 cups cubed meat or seafood
2 cups cooked vegetables
½ cup topping — such as grated Parmesan cheese, parsley, sliced green onion, crumbled bacon or sliced almonds

WHITE SAUCE

- chipped beef, artichoke hearts, mushrooms and green onion
- diced turkey, mushrooms, asparagus and sliced almonds
- chicken, broccoli and crumbled bacon

VELOUTE SAUCE

- chicken, asparagus, mushrooms and almonds
- sausage, leeks, mushrooms and Asiago cheese
- diced turkey, celery, onion, broccoli and parsley

CHEESE SAUCE

- cheddar, broccoli, chicken and bacon
- Swiss, tuna, peas and green onion
- cheddar, beef, broccoli and almonds

Each recipe is sufficient for 4 potatoes.

A POTATO BAR PARTY

A great way to entertain a large group of people and keep your budget in line is a a potato bar party. Serve a big tossed green salad, wine or beer and soft drinks with fresh fruit or sherbet for dessert. It's festive and fun for football games, family reunions and casual get-togethers.

Select one potato per person and add a few extras just in case. A 12- or 13-ounce potato is a good size for a full meal. Wash well and pierce the skin with a fork to prevent bursting. Place potatoes in a single layer on a baking sheet. Bake at 425° for 1 hour. Squeeze gently to make sure potatoes are cooked through. Potatoes may be held in a low oven for 15 minutes before serving. Potatoes may be kept warm in an ice chest lined with bath towels, too!

To serve, place potatoes in a basket lined with colorful napkins. Arrange dishes of condiments nearby so that guests can help themselves. If you are entertaining a large crowd it's best to arrange your buffet so that you can approach it from both sides of the table. Prepare all the toppings and sauces in advance, cover and refrigerate. Here are some topping ideas to get you started:

VEGETABLES

- sliced fresh or sautéed mushrooms
- chopped onions
- sliced green onions
- chives
- steamed broccoli
- steamed cauliflower
- steamed green beans
- shredded carrots
- chopped red or green bell peppers
- sliced olives
- sprouts

DAIRY

- crumbled blue cheese
- butter
- sour cream
- plain yogurt
- cottage cheese
- grated Parmesan cheese
- whipped cream cheese with chives
- grated cheeses

MEATS

- bacon bits
- diced ham
- taco meat
- diced chicken or turkey
- shrimp

SAUCES

- chili
- barbecue
- pizza

- guacamole
- hot cheese sauce
- salsa

MISCELLANEOUS

- nuts
- croutons
- Chinese noodles

- sunflower seeds
- sesame seeds

FAMILY FAVORITES

SLOPPY JOE SPUDS

Servings: 4

Kids love these!

4 potatoes, baked and blossomed
1 lb. ground chuck
1 cup chopped onion
2 cloves garlic, minced
1 green bell pepper, chopped
1 can (15 oz.) tomato sauce
½ cup water

1 tsp. dried thyme
¼ cup catsup
1 tbs. cider vinegar
1 tsp. Worcestershire sauce
¼ tsp. Tabasco Sauce
salt and pepper to taste

In a large skillet over medium high heat, cook meat, onion, garlic and green pepper until meat is browned and vegetables are soft. Drain off any excess fat. Add remaining ingredients and simmer for 10 minutes. Taste and correct seasoning. Divide evenly over prepared potatoes.

POPEYE'S FAVORITE

Servings: 4

For a version that's lower in calories, omit the cheese sauce. Residual heat from the other ingredients is enough to cook the spinach.

4 potatoes, baked and blossomed
1 tbs. oil
1 clove garlic, minced
2 cups diced ham
2 tomatoes, seeded and chopped
½ small bunch spinach
2 cups cheese sauce, page 21
¼ cup grated Parmesan cheese

In a skillet over medium high heat, sauté garlic in oil until soft. Add ham and tomatoes and cook through. Prepare spinach. Remove any large stems and discard. Wash spinach well and shake dry. Stack leaves and roll in a paper towel to blot excess moisture. Slice into ¼-inch slices crosswise. Add spinach to pan and cook briefly until just wilted. Add cheese sauce and heat ingredients together. Taste and correct seasoning. Divide evenly over prepared potatoes. Sprinkle with Parmesan.

CONFETTI EGGS AND HAM

Servings: 4

A nice entrée for brunch. Add a fresh fruit salad and pastry to complete your menu.

4 potatoes, baked and blossomed
2 tbs. oil
1/2 cup chopped onion
1/2 cup chopped green bell pepper
1/4 cup sliced fresh mushrooms
2 tbs. chopped fresh parsley
1 cup diced cooked ham
1 1/2 tsp. salt

1/2 tsp. pepper
1 tsp. Worcestershire sauce
2 tomatoes, seeded and chopped
2 tbs. butter
4 eggs
2 tbs. grated Parmesan cheese
salt and pepper to taste

Heat oil in a large skillet. Over medium high heat, sauté onion until soft. Add green pepper, mushrooms, parsley, ham and seasonings. Cook until pepper is tender-crisp. Add tomatoes to heat through. In a separate pan, heat butter and softly scramble eggs. Divide eggs evenly on top of prepared potatoes. Top with vegetable mixture and sprinkle with Parmesan.

BAKED PORK WITH OLD-FASHIONED BBQ SAUCE

This is one of those cozy winter dinners that everyone loves.

4 potatoes, baked and blossomed
1 lb. boneless pork shoulder
2 tbs. salad oil
1 onion, chopped
1/2 cup chopped celery
2 tbs. cider vinegar
2 tbs. brown sugar

1 cup catsup
3 tbs. Worcestershire sauce
1/2 tsp. dry mustard
1/2 cup water
1/4 tsp. salt
1/4 tsp. pepper

Cut pork into 1-inch cubes and trim off any fat. In a heavy ovenproof skillet over medium high heat, cook pork cubes in oil until evenly browned. In a food processor or blender, combine remaining ingredients for sauce. Pour off any excess fat in skillet. Add sauce to skillet and stir well. Bake mixture in a 325° oven for 1 hour or until pork is very tender. Divide evenly over prepared potatoes.

POTATOES BURGUNDY

Try one of the exotic mushroom varieties — shiitake, chantrelle, enoki, or oyster mushrooms — instead of the traditional domestic mushrooms.

4 potatoes, baked and blossomed
¼ cup butter, divided
1 lb. top round steak, thinly sliced
salt and pepper to taste
2 medium onions, thinly sliced
1 lb. mushrooms, sliced
½ cup burgundy
1 cup shredded Swiss cheese

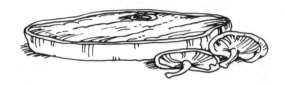

Melt 2 tbs. of butter in a heavy skillet over high heat. Quickly stir-fry meat until done to your liking. Sprinkle with salt and pepper, remove from pan with a slotted spoon and set aside. Add 1 tbs. butter to pan drippings and sauté onions until golden. Remove and set aside. Add remaining butter to pan and cook mushrooms until tender. Add wine and heat through. Return onion and meat to pan. Divide mixture evenly over prepared potatoes. Top with cheese and set under broiler until cheese melts.

STROGANOFF SPUDS

Our kitchen is never without parsley. It adds flavor and just the right bit of color to so many dishes. To store, rinse a large bunch of parsley well under cold running water, and shake to remove excess moisture. Wrap with paper towels and put the wrapped parsley into a glass jar. Cover tightly with the lid and place in the refrigerator where it will keep nicely for a week or more.

4 potatoes, baked and blossomed
1 lb. top sirloin
2 tbs. butter
2 tbs. oil
1 onion, peeled and halved lengthwise
1 clove garlic, minced

8 oz. fresh mushrooms, quartered
1 cup *Demi-Glace*, page 18
2 tbs. catsup or tomato paste
salt and pepper to taste
1 cup sour cream
1 tbs. finely minced parsley

Partially freeze meat. Cut into ¼-inch strips using a sharp knife. Heat butter and oil in a large skillet over medium high heat. Cook meat in 2 batches until browned and tender. Remove and set aside. Cut onion into slivers, add to pan with garlic and cook until tender. Add mushrooms and cook until light brown. Return meat to pan. Add Demi-Glace, catsup, salt and pepper. Cook to heat through. Stir in sour cream, but do not boil. Divide evenly over prepared potatoes and sprinkle with parsley.

CHICKEN AND SAUSAGE

Servings: 4

Serve with a big green salad with red and green peppers and a tangy vinaigrette. To seed a tomato, cut in half horizontally and squeeze each half, cut side down, over the sink.

4 potatoes, baked and blossomed
2 tbs. butter
1 whole chicken breast, skinned, boned and cut into 1-inch cubes
1 clove garlic, minced
salt and pepper to taste
¼ lb. mushrooms

½ lb. Italian link sausage, cut into 1-inch slices
1 cup white wine
1 tomato, seeded and diced
½ tsp. crushed red pepper flakes
½ cup grated Parmesan cheese

Heat butter in a skillet over medium heat, add chicken and garlic and stir fry until chicken is cooked through. Sprinkle with salt and pepper. Remove and set aside. Add mushrooms to skillet and cook until tender. Remove and set aside. Add sausage and cover with white wine. Boil gently until sausage is done. Return chicken and mushrooms to skillet, add tomato and red pepper flakes and heat through. Divide evenly over prepared potatoes and sprinkle with Parmesan.

CHICKEN TETRAZZINI

Servings: 4

This mixture is traditionally served over spaghetti but it is rich, delicious and comforting served over a fluffy baked potato.

4 potatoes, baked and blossomed
3 tbs. butter
3 tbs. flour
1 cup chicken broth
½ cup cream
salt and white pepper to taste
2 cups diced cooked chicken, preferably white meat
¼ cup sliced mushrooms
¼ cup dry sherry
pinch of freshly grated nutmeg
¼ cup grated Parmesan cheese

Melt butter in a medium saucepan, whisk in flour and cook for 2 minutes, stirring constantly. Add chicken broth and cream and bring to a boil. Add salt and pepper, chicken, mushrooms, sherry and nutmeg. Simmer 5 minutes. Taste and correct seasoning. Divide evenly over prepared potatoes and sprinkle with Parmesan.

CHICKEN AND CREAM CHEESE

Servings: 4

Rich and delicious! Garnish with sliced green onions, black olives, salsa and cilantro for real south-of-the-border flair.

4 potatoes, baked and blossomed
2 tbs. butter
1 large onion, sliced
2 cups diced cooked chicken
8 oz. cream cheese, at room temperature
1 can (4 oz.) chopped green chiles
1/4 cup chopped pimiento
1/2 cup milk
salt and pepper to taste
1 cup shredded cheddar cheese
sliced green onions, black olives, salsa and cilantro for garnish

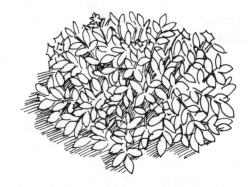

Heat butter in a large skillet and cook onion until golden. Add chicken and cream cheese, cut into cubes. Stir gently until cream cheese begins to melt. Add chiles and pimiento and thin with milk as needed. Season to taste and divide evenly over prepared potatoes. Sprinkle with cheddar and garnish with suggested condiments.

KENTUCKY HOT BROWN

Servings: 4

A famous hotel in Louisville, Kentucky serves a special sandwich called "Hot Brown." This potato topping is a variation of that dish. Serve with broiled tomatoes.

4 potatoes, baked and blossomed
12 slices bacon
2 tbs. minced shallots or onion
3 tbs. flour
1¼ cups milk
1 tsp. Worcestershire sauce
⅛ tsp. cayenne pepper

⅛ tsp. dry mustard
1 tbs. sherry
4 oz. sharp cheddar, shredded
2-3 cups diced cooked chicken or turkey breast
4 tbs. grated Parmesan cheese

Cook bacon in a large skillet until crisp. Remove bacon and drain on paper towels. Discard all but 3 tbs. of bacon drippings. In drippings, sauté shallots until soft. Whisk in flour and cook over medium heat until thickened. Gradually add milk and continue to whisk until bubbly. Add Worcestershire, cayenne, mustard and sherry. Slowly add cheese, stirring continuously. (Tip: always stir in one direction only and your sauces will be much smoother.) Add diced chicken to sauce and heat through. Divide sauce evenly over prepared potatoes and sprinkle with crumbled bacon and Parmesan. Set briefly under the broiler until bubbly.

CHICKEN LIVERS IN CREAM

If you love chicken livers, this dish is for you.

4 potatoes, baked and blossomed
¼ cup butter
1 lb. chicken livers
1 tbs. minced shallots
2 tbs. cognac
1 cup heavy cream
salt and pepper to taste
2 tbs. finely chopped parsley

Rinse chicken livers and pat dry with paper towels. Cut each liver in half. In a large skillet over medium heat, melt butter and sauté livers and shallots. Push mixture to side of pan and add cognac. Ignite. Allow flames to subside. Stir in cream and season to taste with salt and pepper. Divide evenly over prepared potatoes and sprinkle with parsley.

LAMB GRAVY

Servings: 4

For those who like lamb, this is real comfort food. Fix it for dinner some cold, rainy evening when you've had a rough day.

4 potatoes, baked and blossomed
1 lb. ground lamb
2 tbs. butter
1 clove garlic, minced
1 small onion, chopped
salt and pepper to taste
1/2 tsp. rosemary
2 cups brown gravy

In a skillet over medium high heat, brown lamb until no longer pink. Drain and set aside. Heat butter and sauté garlic and onion until soft. Return lamb to skillet and season with salt, pepper and rosemary. Stir in gravy and heat through. Divide evenly over prepared potatoes.

JOE'S SPECIAL

Servings: 4

Practically everyone has had this popular dish using eggs. For a change try it as a topping on a baked potato.

4 potatoes, baked and blossomed
1 lb. lean ground beef
2 tbs. oil
1 medium onion, chopped
2 cloves garlic, minced
1 cup sliced mushrooms
1 pkg. (10 oz.) frozen chopped spinach, thawed
¼ tsp. nutmeg
¼ tsp. oregano
salt and pepper to taste
½ cup grated Parmesan cheese

In a large skillet, brown beef in oil over medium high heat. Add onion and garlic and cook until tender. Stir in mushrooms and cook until soft. Place spinach in a dishtowel and wring tightly to remove liquid. Add to skillet and heat through. Season to taste. Divide evenly over prepared potatoes and sprinkle with Parmesan.

VEAL PARMIGIANA

Servings: 4

Strips of chicken breast also work well in this recipe. There are a number of excellent spaghetti sauces available at the grocery store and in this busy modern day they make wonderful substitutes for homemade.

4 potatoes, baked and blossomed
2 tbs. olive oil
8 oz. veal, cut in thin strips
1 green bell pepper, cored and coarsely
  chopped
8 oz. mushrooms, sliced

1 clove garlic, minced
salt and black pepper to taste
2 cups spaghetti sauce
1 cup shredded mozzarella cheese
2 lbs. grated Parmesan cheese

Heat olive oil in a large skillet over medium high heat. Add veal and quickly stir-fry until light golden brown, about 3 minutes. Remove and set aside. Add pepper to pan and cook until softened, add mushrooms and garlic and cook until tender. Season to taste. Add spaghetti sauce and bring to a simmer. Add veal and heat through. Divide mixture evenly over prepared potatoes. Top with cheeses and broil briefly to melt.

PORK AND APPLE TOPPING

Servings: 4

The richness of pork complements the sweet potatoes in this tasty topping. It also goes well on regular baked potatoes or brown rice.

4 sweet potatoes or yams, baked and
   blossomed
1 lb. pork tenderloin
3 tbs. flour
1/4 tsp. pepper
2 tbs. sherry
1 tbs. low sodium soy sauce

1 tsp. cider vinegar
1/4 tsp. ground coriander seed
4 tbs. oil, divided
1 medium onion, sliced
1 Granny Smith apple, peeled, cored, sliced
1 red bell pepper, cored and diced
1 clove garlic, minced

Cut pork into thin slices across the grain. Combine flour and pepper in a plastic bag. Shake pork strips in flour until coated. Combine sherry, soy, vinegar and coriander in a small bowl and set aside. Heat 2 tbs. of oil in a large skillet over medium high heat. Cook pork strips until browned and crispy, about 3 minutes. Remove from pan and set aside. Add remaining 2 tbs. of oil to skillet and cook onion until tender. Add apple, pepper and garlic and stir-fry for 2 minutes. Return pork to pan, add sherry mixture and stir until heated through. Divide evenly over prepared potatoes.

QUICK CHILI POTATOES

Servings: 4

This streamlined recipe can be frozen and reheated in the microwave for a quick winter dinner. It's ideal for those times when everyone is on a different schedule and has plans for the evening.

4 potatoes, baked and blossomed
1 lb. ground chuck
1 cup chopped onion
2 cloves garlic, minced
1 green bell pepper, chopped
1 can (16 oz.) crushed tomatoes in
   puree
1 can (16 oz.) kidney beans, drained
1-2 tbs. chili powder

1 tsp. cumin
1 tsp. oregano
½ tsp. Tabasco Sauce
½ tsp. pepper
salt to taste
sour cream, shredded cheddar cheese,
   chopped onion for garnish, optional

In a large skillet over medium high heat, cook beef with onion, garlic and green pepper until meat is no longer pink and vegetables are soft. Drain off any excess juices. Add tomatoes, beans and seasonings. Simmer for 20 minutes, adding water if mixture becomes too thick. Divide evenly over prepared potatoes and garnish as desired.

CHILI BLANCO

This chili is "New Wave" as it uses ground turkey and pink beans instead of the more traditional ingredients.

4 potatoes, baked and blossomed
2 tbs. oil
1 lb. ground turkey
1 large onion, chopped
2 cloves garlic, minced
2 tbs. chili powder
2 tsp. cumin
1 tsp. dried oregano
salt and pepper to taste

1 can (4 oz.) can chopped green chiles
1 can (16 oz.) crushed tomatoes in
  puree
1 can (16 oz.) chicken broth
1 can (16 oz.) pink kidney beans
sour cream, cubed avocado, salsa,
  shredded cheddar, cilantro, lime
  wedges for garnish, optional

Heat oil in a large skillet over medium high heat. Cook turkey, onion and garlic until turkey is light brown and onion is soft. Drain off excess fat or juices. Add remaining ingredients and simmer 30 minutes. Season to taste. Divide evenly over prepared potatoes and garnish as desired.

PORK AND BLACK BEAN CHILI

In this health-conscious society, black beans have come in to their own. We buy them at the health food store and simmer a batch for a black beans and rice salad or this unusual chili. It's easy to double the recipe and it freezes well. Delicious on potatoes or rice, it also makes a great filling for tortillas.

4 potatoes, baked and blossomed
1½ lb. boneless pork loin or shoulder
3 tbs. oil
1 large onion, chopped
2 cloves garlic, minced
2 tsp. ground cumin
2 tbs. chili powder
2 tsp. dried oregano

salt and pepper to taste
2 cans (16 oz. each) crushed tomatoes
 in puree
3 cups cooked black beans
sour cream, shredded cheddar, diced
 red onion, avocado cubes, cilantro for
 garnish, optional

Chill pork until very cold. Trim off fat. Cut pork into ½-inch dice. Heat oil in a large skillet over medium heat. Add pork and cook, stirring frequently until pork is no longer pink. Add onion and garlic; cook until onion is softened and pork is browned. Stir in remaining ingredients and simmer for 30 minutes. If mixture becomes too thick, add water. Season to taste. Divide evenly over prepared potatoes and garnish as desired.

INTERNATIONAL FAVORITES

PORK FAJITA TOPPING

Servings: 4

Chicken, beef or shrimp are also excellent when prepared in this manner.

4 potatoes, baked and blossomed
4 center-cut boneless pork chops
1 tsp. chili powder
1 tsp. ground cumin
1 clove garlic, minced
1/4 tsp. cayenne pepper
1/2 tsp. salt
2 tbs. salad oil

1 large green bell pepper, cut into strips
1 white onion, cut into quarters
1/2 cup sour cream
1/2 cup salsa
1 avocado, diced
1 tbs. chopped cilantro
1 lime, cut into wedges

Cut pork chops into 1/4-inch-thick strips. Combine chili powder, cumin, garlic, cayenne and salt in a plastic bag. Add pork and shake well to coat meat. Refrigerate several hours or overnight. Heat oil in a large skillet and sauté green pepper over very high heat until tender. Some of the pieces should be a bit charred. remove and set aside. Cut onion quarters into strips and stir-fry strips until tender. Remove and add to peppers. Turn heat to medium, adding more oil if necessary. Cook pork strips until tender and no longer pink. Add pepper and onion mixture to pan and heat through. Divide evenly over prepared potatoes and top with sour cream, salsa, diced avocado and cilantro. Serve with wedges of lime to squeeze over the top.

MEXICAN CALIENTE CHEESE SAUCE

Servings: 4

Arrange bowls of halved cherry tomatoes, sliced ripe olives, avocado cubes, sliced green onions and salsa in the center of the table so each person can top his potato as he wishes.

4 potatoes, baked and blossomed
1 lb. Monterey Jack cheese, shredded
1/2 lb. sharp cheddar, shredded
1/4 cup flour
1 can (12 oz.) beer
1 clove garlic, minced
1 can (4 oz.) chopped green chilies
3 tsp. chili powder
cayenne to taste

Shred cheeses and toss in a large bowl with flour. In a large saucepan, heat beer over medium high heat. Add garlic, slowly stir in cheese by the handful, and using a wooden spoon stir constantly in one direction only. When all the cheese has been added, stir in green chilies, chili powder and cayenne to taste. Divide hot cheese sauce evenly over prepared potatoes.

CABO SAN LUCAS TOPPING

Servings: 4

This flavorful topping reminds us of the sunny flavors of Mexico.

4 potatoes, baked and blossomed
1 cup sour cream
½ cup salsa
2 tbs. oil
1 clove garlic, minced
2 whole chicken breasts, skinned, boned and diced
1 cup shredded jalapeño cheese
1 avocado, peeled, pitted and diced
1 tomato, seeded and diced
½ cup chopped red onion
1 tbs. chopped cilantro, optional

Combine sour cream and salsa in a small bowl. Heat oil and sauté garlic until soft. Add chicken and stir-fry until cooked through. Divide evenly over prepared potatoes and top with sour cream sauce. Sprinkle with cheese and top with avocado, tomato, red onion and cilantro.

CHIMICHANGA TOPPING

Servings: 8

This recipe is ideal for using leftovers — beef pot roast, pork, turkey or chicken — you'll need about 3 cups. Leftover filling freezes well.

8 potatoes, baked and blossomed
3 cups shredded meat or poultry
1 jar (16 oz.) salsa
1 can (16 oz.) refried beans
1 can (4 oz.) diced green chilies
1 envelope taco seasoning
8 oz. shredded cheddar or Monterey Jack cheese
additional salsa, sour cream, diced tomatoes, sliced green onions,
   sliced black olives for garnish

In a large skillet over medium heat, combine meat, salsa, beans, undrained chilies and taco seasoning. Stir gently to heat through. Divide evenly over prepared potatoes, top with cheese and garnish as desired.

BEEF AND BREW SPUDS

Servings: 4

The flavors of this topping will remind you of merry old England. The Cordon Bleu insists you ALWAYS use dry mustard with cheese!

4 potatoes, baked and blossomed
1 can (12 oz.) beer
1 lb. sharp cheddar cheese, shredded
⅓ cup flour
1 tsp. Worcestershire sauce
salt to taste
cayenne to taste
½ tsp. dry mustard
8 oz. rare deli roast beef, cut into strips
parsley sprigs for garnish

In a heavy saucepan, bring beer to a gentle boil over medium heat. In a large bowl, toss shredded cheese with flour to coat. Using a wooden spoon to stir constantly, gradually add cheese, a handful at a time, until all cheese has been added. Stir in one direction only. Add seasonings to taste. Stir in roast beef and heat through. Divide evenly over prepared potatoes and garnish with parsley.

BEEF SZECHWAN

Dark sesame oil adds a great deal of flavor to Oriental dishes. Be sure to keep it in the refrigerator so it won't turn rancid. Fresh ginger is easy to prepare using the food processor. Finely chop a large root and freeze what you don't need for later.

4 potatoes, baked and blossomed
1 lb. flank steak
2 tbs. low sodium soy sauce
4 tsp. sesame oil, divided
1½ tsp. sugar
1 tsp. cornstarch
2 cloves garlic, minced
1 tbs. minced ginger
¼ tsp. crushed red pepper flakes
1 red bell pepper, cored and cut into strips
1 pkg. (8 oz.) baby corn, thawed
¼ lb. snow peas, halved on the diagonal
¼ cup green onions, thinly sliced on the diagonal

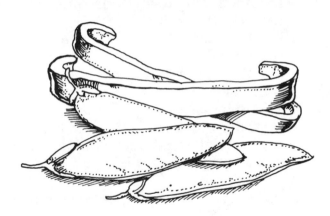

Cut steak in half lengthwise. Slice across the grain into ¼-inch strips. Combine soy, 2 tsp. sesame oil, sugar and cornstarch. Place meat in a plastic bag and add soy mixture, coating meat well. Refrigerate if not cooking immediately. Heat 2 tsp. sesame oil in a large skillet over medium high heat. Stir-fry aromatics — garlic, ginger and crushed red pepper flakes — for 30 seconds. Add red bell pepper and corn and stir-fry 2 minutes. Add snow peas and cook until tender and bright green. Remove vegetables from skillet and set aside. Add beef strips to skillet and stir-fry until tender, 2 to 3 minutes. Return vegetables to skillet and heat through. Divide evenly over prepared potatoes and sprinkle with green onions.

CHICKEN TERIYAKI

Servings: 4

For a simple and unusual garnish, place four green onions in the microwave and cook on high for 60 seconds. Cool under cold water and tie each onion into a knot. Trim ends evenly with scissors. You'll have people wondering...

4 potatoes, baked and blossomed
1/2 cup soy sauce
1/2 cup dark brown sugar
1 clove garlic, minced
2 tbs. freshly grated ginger
4 chicken thighs, skinned, boned and
  cubed

2 tbs. oil
1/4 lb. snow peas
1/4 cup sliced green onions
1/2 cup chopped cashews

Combine soy, sugar, garlic and ginger in a small bowl. Place chicken in a plastic zip lock bag and pour marinade over. Refrigerate several hours or overnight. Heat 2 tbs. oil in a skillet over medium high heat. Drain chicken and stir-fry until chicken is almost done. Add snow peas and cook until tender-crisp and bright green. If mixture becomes too dry, add a bit more marinade. Divide mixture evenly over prepared potatoes and sprinkle with green onions and cashews.

HOT AND SOUR SHRIMP

Servings: 4

Add the red pepper flakes to suit your personal taste for heat. This quick stir-fry is also low in calories. Try using shiitake mushrooms for a change of pace.

4 potatoes, baked and blossomed
2 tbs. low sodium soy sauce
2 tbs. rice vinegar
1 tsp. sugar
1/4 to 1/2 tsp. crushed red pepper flakes
2 cloves garlic, minced
1 tsp. dark sesame oil

1 lb. medium shrimp, peeled
1 tbs. oil
4 green onions, cut on the diagonal
   into 2-inch lengths
8 oz. fresh mushrooms, sliced
2 cups snow peas, trimmed and sliced
   in half diagonally

Combine soy, vinegar, sugar, crushed red pepper flakes, garlic and sesame oil. Marinate shrimp in mixture for several hours or overnight. Heat oil in a large skillet over medium high heat. Sauté green onions for 1 minute; add mushrooms and cook for 2 minutes longer. Add snow peas and cook for 1 minute. Pour shrimp and marinade into skillet and stir-fry for 2 minutes or until shrimp turns pink. Divide evenly over prepared potatoes.

PAELLA POTATOES

All the tasty ingredients which go into the famous Spanish dish, paella, are served on top of a potato.

4 potatoes, baked and blossomed
4 tbs. olive oil, divided
2 cloves garlic, minced
1 onion, chopped
1 tsp. turmeric
1 chicken breast, skinned, boned, cubed
4 oz. Italian sausage links, cut on the
  diagonal in 1/2-inch slices

1/2 green bell pepper, cut in 1/2-inch dice
1 tomato, seeded and chopped into
  1/2-inch dice
1/2 cup frozen green peas
4 oz. medium shrimp with tails
salt and pepper to taste

Heat 2 tbs. of olive oil in a large skillet over medium high heat. Add garlic and onion and sauté until softened. Sprinkle with turmeric. Remove and set aside. Add chicken cubes to skillet and cook until opaque. Remove and set aside. Add sausage and cook through. Drain off fat. Add green pepper and tomato and cook until heated through. Return onion mixture and chicken to skillet. Add peas and shrimp. Cook until shrimp are done and mixture is hot. Season to taste. Divide evenly over prepared potatoes.

PORK PAPRIKASH

When slicing meat for stir-fry dishes, always partially freeze the meat to make sure it is icy cold and use a very sharp knife. It will greatly speed the process.

4 potatoes, baked and blossomed
1 lb. boneless pork loin chops
1 tbs. butter
1 tbs. oil
salt and pepper to taste
3 tsp. Hungarian paprika

2 tbs. finely chopped onion
½ cup white wine
1 cup sour cream
1 tbs. Dijon mustard
1 tbs. minced parsley

Slice pork into ¼-inch strips. Heat butter and oil in a large skillet over medium high heat. Add pork and stir-fry until meat is browned and cooked through. Sprinkle meat with salt and pepper, remove from skillet and set aside. Add paprika and onion to skillet and cook until onion is soft. Stir in white wine, sour cream and mustard and whisk until blended and smooth. Do not boil. Return pork to skillet and heat through. Divide evenly over prepared potatoes and garnish with parsley.

JERKED CHICKEN

Servings: 4

This is Caribbean in origin. Try it on a baked sweet potato or yam for an authentic island treat. You can use pork as well as chicken. Be sure to wear plastic gloves when handling the jalapeño and be careful of your eyes.

4 sweet potatoes or yams, baked and blossomed
2 chicken breasts, skinned, boned and cubed

MARINADE

½ cup sliced green onion
1 fresh jalapeño chile, finely diced
1 tbs. soy
1 tbs. lime juice
1 tsp. ground allspice
½ tsp. dry mustard
½ bay leaf, finely crumbled
1 clove garlic, minced
1 tsp. salt
½ tsp. thyme
¼ tsp. cinnamon

Combine marinade ingredients and pour over prepared chicken in a plastic bag. Refrigerate for several hours or overnight. Chicken mixture may be stir- fried or grilled but grilling is more authentic. To stir-fry, heat 2 tbs. oil in a skillet over medium heat, add chicken and cook 3 to 4 minutes or until cooked through. To grill, soak wooden skewers in water for 1 hour. Thread chicken onto skewers and grill, turning once, until chicken is cooked through. Divide mixture evenly over prepared potatoes.

PINEAPPLE SALSA

Makes: 1¼ cups

*Serve with **Jerked Chicken**.*

1 can (8 oz.) crushed pineapple in juice
¼ cup chopped red onion
1 jalapeño chile, minced
¼ cup chopped fresh cilantro
2 tsp. lime juice
1 tsp. red wine vinegar
¼ tsp. salt

Combine all ingredients and chill.

REUBEN MURPHYS

Purchase corned beef at your deli to make preparation a cinch.

4 potatoes, baked and blossomed
1 tbs. butter
1 onion, chopped
8 oz. deli corned beef

1 can (16 oz.) sauerkraut
1 cup *Russian Dressing*, follows
4 oz. Swiss cheese, shredded
2 tsp. caraway seeds, optional

Melt butter in a skillet and cook onion until soft. Cut corned beef into strips. Drain sauerkraut well and add to skillet with corned beef. Heat mixture through. Divide mixture evenly over potatoes, top with dressing and sprinkle with cheese. Broil briefly to melt cheese. If desired, sprinkle with caraway seeds.

RUSSIAN DRESSING

1 cup mayonnaise
2 tbs. chili sauce
2 tbs. dill pickles, chopped

2 tsp. lemon juice
2 tsp. sugar

Combine ingredients in a small bowl.

TURKISH TOPPING

The fluffy white potato, spicy meat mixture and crisp, cool vegetables create an appealing contrast in temperature and texture.

4 potatoes, baked and blossomed
½ lb. ground chuck
½ lb. ground lamb
½ cup finely chopped onion
1 clove garlic, minced
½ cup catsup
2 tbs. chopped parsley
1 tsp. dried oregano leaves

1 tsp. cinnamon
½ tsp. ground cumin
¼ tsp. cloves
1 tsp. salt
½ tsp. pepper
1 green bell pepper, cored and chopped
2 plum tomatoes, sliced
1 small red onion, halved and slivered

In a large skillet over medium high heat, cook meats, onion and garlic until onion is soft and meat is no longer pink. Drain off excess fat and add catsup, herbs and spices. Simmer 5 minutes. Divide meat mixture evenly over prepared potatoes and garnish with green pepper, plum tomatoes and red onion.

GREEK TOPPING WITH CUCUMBER YOGURT SAUCE

The meat can be marinated the day before and the sauce prepared and refrigerated. Serve with a big green salad with crumbled feta cheese and Greek olives. A simple and quick trick for pitting olives: place them on a cutting board, and using a broad-bladed chef's knife, give the blade a quick slam with your fist. Under certain circumstances, this can also be good therapy for the cook!

4 potatoes, baked and blossomed
1 lb. lean boneless pork
¼ cup olive oil
¼ cup lemon juice
2 tbs. Dijon mustard
2 cloves garlic, minced
1½ tsp. crumbled oregano
1 tsp. crumbled thyme
1 tbs. olive oil
Cucumber Yogurt Sauce, follows
1 tomato, seeded and diced, for garnish
½ small red onion, thinly sliced, for garnish

Trim fat from pork. Place in freezer for 30 minutes to facilitate slicing. Slice into thin bite-sized strips. Place pork in a heavy duty plastic bag. In a small bowl, combine oil, lemon juice, mustard, garlic and herbs, mixing well. Pour over pork and mix well. Refrigerate for at least 6 hours or overnight.

To make topping, drain pork and discard marinade. Heat a large skillet and add 1 tbs. oil. Stir-fry pork over medium high heat until cooked through, about 3 minutes. Divide evenly over prepared potatoes. Garnish with *Cucumber Yogurt Sauce*, tomato and onion.

CUCUMBER YOGURT SAUCE

8 oz. plain yogurt
1 cup diced cucumber, peeled and seeded
1 tsp. dill
½ tsp. seasoned salt
1 clove garlic, minced

Combine ingredients and chill.

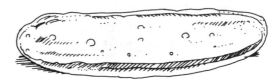

TASTE OF ITALY TOPPING

Servings: 4

This version is vegetarian, but cooked Italian sausage, slivers of salami, pepperoni or other Italian meats would be nice additions.

4 potatoes, baked and blossomed
1 jar (6 oz.) marinated artichoke hearts, drained, marinade reserved
1 clove garlic, minced
3 Italian plum tomatoes, coarsely chopped
1/4 cup sliced ripe olives
1 tbs. chopped fresh parsley
1 tsp. crumbled oregano
1 cup shredded provolone cheese

Pour marinade into a skillet and sauté garlic over medium high heat until soft. Add artichokes, tomatoes and olives and heat through. Sprinkle with herbs. Divide evenly into prepared potatoes and sprinkle with cheese.

GREEK TAVERNA TOPPING

Servings: 4

Cinnamon, allspice and tomato give this topping an unusual Greek flavor. Use leftover dark turkey meat or ground turkey.

4 potatoes, baked and blossomed
2 tbs. olive oil
1 small onion, chopped
1 clove garlic, minced
1 small carrot, finely diced
2 cups shredded dark turkey meat or cooked ground turkey
1 cup tomato sauce
1/2 cup robust red wine
1 bay leaf
1 tsp. cinnamon
1/4 tsp. ground allspice
1/4 tsp. crushed red pepper flakes
1/2 tsp. ground black pepper

In a heavy skillet, heat olive oil. Sauté onion until soft. Add garlic and carrot and cook for 3 minutes, stirring over medium high heat. Add remaining ingredients and simmer for 30 minutes. Remove bay leaf and divide evenly over prepared potatoes.

ITALIAN SAUSAGE SAUTÉ

Servings: 4

There's a wonderful variety of Italian sausages on the market. Use hot, sweet or a combination of your favorites for this topping. Be sure to prick the skin in several places to allow the grease to escape and to keep sausages from bursting.

4 potatoes, baked and blossomed
1 lb. Italian sausages
1 cup red wine or water
2 tbs. olive oil
1 clove garlic, minced

1 large onion, thinly sliced
1 green bell pepper, thinly sliced
2 cups spaghetti sauce
4 oz. mozzarella cheese, shredded
2 tbs. grated Parmesan cheese

Place sausages in a large skillet and add wine or water. Simmer over medium heat for 10 minutes, turning occasionally. Remove sausages to a cutting board and cut into ½-inch slices. Wipe out skillet and add oil. Sauté garlic and onion until limp. Add sausage slices and green bell pepper and cook until sausages are light brown and pepper is softened. Add spaghetti sauce and heat through. Divide mixture evenly over prepared potatoes. Top with cheeses and broil briefly to melt.

CHICKEN ROMA

Sometimes there's confusion between shredded Parmesan and grated Parmesan. Grated Parmesan is the almost powdered variety that you can grate yourself, or that comes in cans. We don't use canned Parmesan often, but find it works best in sauces where smoothness is desired. The shredded is what we use most in salads and as a topping. It adds more personality and visual appeal to the finished dish. And of course, <u>freshly</u> grated or shredded is always the most flavorful!

4 potatoes, baked and blossomed
2 chicken breasts, skinned, boned and
  cubed
1 clove garlic, minced
1 cup mushrooms, sliced

1 small onion, diced
1 small jar marinated artichoke hearts,
  drained, marinade reserved
1 cup tomato or spaghetti sauce
¼ cup shredded Parmesan cheese

Pour artichoke marinade into a skillet and sauté chicken over medium heat until cooked through. Remove and set aside. Sauté garlic and onion until soft. Add mushrooms and cook until limp. Coarsely chop artichoke hearts. Stir into mixture together with tomato sauce and heat through. Divide evenly over prepared potatoes and sprinkle with Parmesan.

SEAFOOD TOPPINGS

POTATOES PRIMAVERA

Pass extra shredded Parmesan to go on top.

4 potatoes, baked and blossomed
1 cup small broccoli florets
1 cup thinly sliced carrots
1 cup fresh green beans, trimmed to
  1½-inch lengths

1 small zucchini, cut in half lengthwise
  and thinly sliced crosswise
1 red pepper, cut into 1½-inch strips
8 oz. medium-size shrimp, peeled and
  deveined

Bring a large pot of water to a boil. Add broccoli, carrots and green beans; cook 4 minutes. Add zucchini and bell pepper and cook 2 minutes longer. Add shrimp and cook until opaque. Pour into a strainer and refresh with cold water to stop cooking process.

Make sauce:

¾ cup heavy cream
½ cup chicken broth

¼ cup grated Parmesan cheese
freshly ground black pepper

Combine sauce ingredients in a small saucepan and cook, over medium heat, stirring constantly until slightly thickened. Add vegetables and shrimp and heat through. Taste and correct seasoning. Pour over prepared potatoes. Sprinkle with freshly ground black pepper and pass additional Parmesan.

SCAMPI MARNIER

Always be careful not to overcook scampi, as it toughens them.

4 potatoes, baked and blossomed
1/4 cup butter
2 cloves garlic, minced
1 lb. fresh scampi
2 tbs. white wine
1 cup prepared pesto
1 cup prepared spaghetti sauce
1/4 cup finely minced fresh parsley

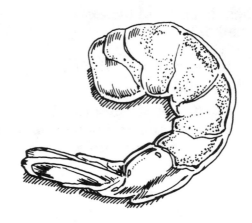

Heat butter in a large skillet over medium high heat. Add garlic and sauté until soft. Add scampi and quickly stir-fry until almost opaque. Add wine, pesto and spaghetti sauce and heat through. Divide evenly over prepared potatoes and sprinkle with parsley.

SEAFOOD PICANTE

People eat first with their eyes, and in Christie's catering business it is strictly forbidden to serve "naked" food. Garnish this dish with lemon wedges and big frills of parsley.

4 potatoes, baked and blossomed
1 tbs. butter
1 cup chopped onion
1 cup chopped green bell pepper
1 cup chopped celery
1 clove garlic, minced
2 cups seeded, chopped fresh tomatoes
1/4 tsp. crushed red pepper flakes
1 bay leaf

1/2 tsp. crumbled thyme
1/2 tsp. oregano leaves
1/4 tsp. crumbled rosemary
1/2 tsp. black pepper
1 cup spaghetti sauce
1/2 lb. bay scallops
1/2 lb. baby shrimp
2 tbs. freshly grated Parmesan cheese

In a large skillet over medium high heat, melt butter and sauté onion, pepper, celery and garlic until tender. Add tomatoes, seasonings and spaghetti sauce and simmer 15 minutes. Add scallops and cook until they turn opaque. Add shrimp and heat through. Divide evenly over prepared potatoes and sprinkle with Parmesan.

SHRIMP MILANESE

If you have fresh basil, it makes a wonderful difference. Thinly snip the leaves into strips, using kitchen scissors. This is called a "chiffonade" and can be used with spinach, sorrel and lettuce as well.

4 potatoes, baked and blossomed
2 tbs. olive oil
1 clove garlic, minced
1 cup sliced mushrooms
2 tomatoes, seeded and chopped
1/4 cup sliced green onion
1/4 cup sliced black olives
1 cup tomato or spaghetti sauce
1 cup cooked baby shrimp
1 tsp. crumbled basil or fresh basil strips
1/4 cup freshly shredded Parmesan cheese

In a skillet, heat oil and sauté garlic over medium high heat until soft. Add mushrooms and cook until tender. Stir in tomatoes and green onion and cook until limp. Add olives, sauce and shrimp and heat through. Divide evenly over prepared potatoes and garnish with basil and Parmesan.

SCALLOPS BERNAISE

Servings: 4

We like the richness a bit of bacon adds to this sauce. Knorr Swiss makes an excellent Bernaise. Asparagus makes a nice side dish.

4 potatoes, baked and blossomed
2 strips bacon, diced
2 green onions, sliced
1 cup sliced mushrooms
8 oz. scallops
2 tbs. white wine
1 pkg. Bernaise sauce mix, prepared per instructions

In a large skillet, sauté bacon until limp. Add green onions and mushrooms and cook until mushrooms are tender. Add scallops and wine and cook until scallops are opaque. Stir in Bernaise and heat through. Do not boil or mixture will curdle. Divide evenly over prepared potatoes.

CIOPINNO POTATOES

A crisp green salad, a glass of wine and you're all set for a feast.

4 large potatoes, baked and blossomed
1 onion, chopped
1 clove garlic, minced
2 tbs. olive oil
1 cup chopped tomatoes in puree
¼ cup white wine
1 tbs. tomato paste
1 tsp. basil
1 tsp. oregano
1 cup crab meat
1 cup cooked baby shrimp
hot pepper sauce and black pepper, to taste

In a medium skillet, sauté onion and garlic in olive oil until softened. Add tomatoes, wine, tomato paste and seasonings. Simmer 15 minutes. Stir in crab meat and shrimp and heat through. Taste and add pepper sauce and black pepper. Divide evenly over prepared potatoes.

CRAB MORNAY

In the Pacific Northwest, we are lucky to get fresh Dungeness crab. It's expensive but worth every penny.

4 potatoes, baked and blossomed
¼ cup butter
4 green onions, finely chopped
¼ cup minced parsley
1 tbs. flour
1 cup cream
1 cup shredded Swiss cheese
1 tbs. sherry
salt and cayenne to taste
12 oz. fresh crab meat

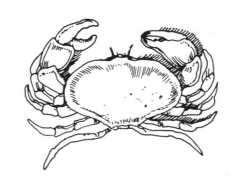

In a saucepan over medium heat, melt butter and sauté onions and parsley until soft. Sprinkle with flour and stir to combine. Add cream and stir until smooth. Slowly add cheese, and stir until melted. Season to taste with sherry, salt and cayenne. Add crab and heat through. Divide evenly over prepared potatoes.

SMOKED SALMON BRUNCH

Servings: 4

This makes a nice lunch or brunch if you use the optional scrambled eggs. Be sure to use only the finest cold smoked salmon or lox. Although it's expensive, a little goes a long way.

4 potatoes, baked and blossomed
1/4 cup butter
1/2 cup thinly sliced green onions
16 slices smoked salmon
salt and pepper to taste
4 eggs, lightly scrambled, optional
1 cup shredded Swiss cheese

Heat butter in a small skillet until foamy. Cook green onions over medium heat until limp. Cut salmon into 1/2-inch strips. Add to pan and cook until heated through. Season to taste. Divide evenly into prepared potatoes and top with scrambled eggs, if desired. Sprinkle evenly with cheese.

LOBSTER AND SHRIMP

Meat from one lobster tail is enough for four servings.

4 potatoes, baked and blossomed
3 tbs. butter
2 tbs. sliced almonds
½ cup sour cream
¼ cup dry vermouth
1 tsp. salt
1 cup sliced cooked lobster (meat from 1 tail)
½ cup cooked baby shrimp

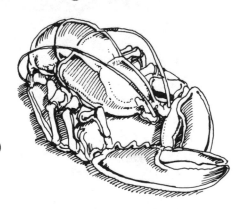

In a medium skillet, melt butter and sauté almonds over medium heat until golden. Remove and set aside. In a small bowl, combine sour cream, vermouth and salt. Add lobster and shrimp to the skillet and stir until heated through. Add sour cream mixture and combine. Divide evenly over prepared potatoes and sprinkle with reserved almonds.

VEGETARIAN AND LOW CALORIE TOPPINGS

CHICKEN VEGETABLE TOPPING

Servings: 4

With the excellent variety of spaghetti sauces now available at the grocery store, it's easy to put together a healthy and delicious potato topping in just minutes. Use any other fresh vegetables you might have on hand — carrots, peas, onions, mushrooms, green beans or celery.

4 potatoes, baked and blossomed
2 tbs. butter
1 yellow summer squash, sliced into 1/2-inch rounds
4 green onions, sliced
1 lb. ground chicken
2 cups spaghetti sauce
salt and pepper to taste
1/2 cup shredded Parmesan cheese

Melt butter and sauté squash in a large skillet over medium high heat until beginning to soften. Add green onions and cook mixture until onion is limp. Remove and set aside. In the same skillet, sauté chicken until it is cooked through. Drain off any juices. Add vegetable mixture and spaghetti sauce. Simmer 10 minutes. Season to taste. Divide evenly over prepared potatoes. Sprinkle with Parmesan.

CHICKEN WITH HERBS

Servings: 4

If you grow your own herbs, this is a great way to add freshness and wonderful flavor, plus it is low in calories.

4 potatoes, baked and blossomed
2 tbs. butter
2 chicken breasts, skinned, boned and cubed
1 clove garlic, minced
10 sprigs parsley, chopped
10 basil leaves, chopped
2 tsp. fresh tarragon, chopped
1 cup chicken broth
1 tbs. Dijon mustard
salt and pepper to taste

Heat butter in a large skillet and stir-fry chicken with garlic until chicken is done. Add herbs and chicken broth. Whisk in mustard and season to taste with salt and pepper. Divide evenly over prepared potatoes.

OYSTER BEEF

Another time, try adding 2 cups of steamed broccoli, asparagus or snow peas to this dish.

4 potatoes, baked and blossomed
1 lb. boneless lean beef, such as sirloin
2 green onions, chopped
2 tbs. low sodium soy sauce
2 tbs. water
1 tbs. cornstarch

1 tbs. white wine
2 tbs. oil
2 tbs. oyster sauce
1 tsp. sugar
toasted sesame seeds for garnish

Partially freeze meat for easier slicing. Slice across the grain into ¼-inch slices. Combine green onions, soy, water, cornstarch and wine in a food processor or in a small bowl. Add meat and stir to coat well. Let stand at room temperature for 15 minutes. Heat 1 tbs. of oil over high heat in a heavy skillet. Cook half the meat at a time, stir-frying in hot skillet until browned, about 2 minutes. Remove and set aside. Repeat with remaining oil and meat. Return meat to skillet and stir in oyster sauce and sugar until combined. Divide evenly over prepared potatoes and sprinkle with sesame seed.

CHICKEN ORIENTAL

Needless to say, this is also good on rice.

4 potatoes, baked and blossomed
1 lb. ground chicken
2 tbs. oil
1 onion, chopped
2 carrots, chopped
2 stalks celery, chopped
1½ cups prepared teriyaki sauce
salt and pepper to taste

In a skillet over medium high heat, cook chicken until crumbly. Remove and set aside. Wipe out pan with paper toweling. Heat oil and sauté onion until soft. Add carrots and celery and cook until tender-crisp. Return chicken to the pan and add teriyaki sauce. Heat through. Taste and correct seasoning. Divide evenly over prepared potatoes.

VEGETABLE SAUTÉ WITH PESTO

Servings: 4

Use any fresh vegetables you have on hand.

4 potatoes, baked and blossomed
2 tbs. oil
1 clove garlic, minced
2 carrots, thinly sliced
2 stalks celery, thinly sliced
1 onion, chopped
1 red bell pepper, sliced
1 zucchini, sliced
8 oz. fresh mushrooms, sliced
½ cup prepared pesto
½ cup shredded Parmesan cheese

Heat oil in a large skillet over medium high heat. Stir-fry garlic, carrots, celery and onion until soft. Add pepper, zucchini and mushrooms and cook until beginning to brown. Stir in pesto. Divide evenly over prepared potatoes and sprinkle with Parmesan.

ZUCCHINI AND CHILE TOPPING

Servings: 4

If your garden is over-zealous in its zucchini production, try this topping.

4 potatoes, baked and blossomed
1 tbs. oil
1 tbs. butter
1 onion, thinly sliced
2 zucchini, sliced ½-inch thick on the diagonal
2 tomatoes, seeded and chopped
1 can (4 oz.) diced green chiles
salt and pepper to taste
1 cup sour cream
1 cup shredded Monterey Jack cheese

In a large skillet over medium high heat, combine oil and butter and sauté onion until soft. Add zucchini and cook until beginning to brown. Add tomatoes and chiles and heat through. Sprinkle with salt and pepper. Stir in sour cream and heat through, but do not boil. Divide evenly over prepared potatoes and sprinkle with cheese. Broil briefly to melt cheese.

VEGGIE POTATO

This is a great way to use leftover vegetables and cheeses. Whenever we're down to the last chunk of cheese, we shred it and put it in a zip lock bag in the freezer. We have quite an assortment of cheeses — Swiss, cheddar, Monterey Jack, havarti — all shredded and ready to go for topping potatoes, pizzas or sandwiches.

4 potatoes, baked and blossomed
1 small onion, chopped
2 tbs. butter
2 cups cooked broccoli florets
1 cup cooked cauliflower florets
1 cup cooked carrot sliced
½ cup ranch dressing
1 cup shredded cheese
¼ cup cooked, crumbled bacon, optional

In a medium skillet, sauté onion in butter until limp. Add vegetables and heat through. Divide evenly over prepared potatoes. Drizzle each with 2 tbs. ranch dressing. Sprinkle with cheese and top with bacon, if desired.

VEGETABLE MELANGE
WITH BALSAMIC VINEGAR

Servings: 4

Balsamic vinegar adds wonderful flavor to so many foods. This makes a light and healthy entrée that's low in fat and high in flavor.

4 potatoes, baked and blossomed
3 tbs. olive oil
2 cloves garlic, minced
1 large onion, chopped
2 small zucchini, sliced into ½-inch rounds
1 cup mushrooms, sliced
¼ cup balsamic vinegar
1 to 2 tsp. sugar
salt and pepper

Heat oil in a skillet over medium high heat. Sauté garlic and onion until soft. Add zucchini and cook until browned on the edges. Add mushrooms and continue cooking until they are soft. Drizzle with vinegar, taste and add sugar to your liking. Divide evenly over prepared potatoes. Sprinkle with salt and pepper to taste.

COMPANY FARE

ARTICHOKES WITH CHAMPAGNE TOPPING Servings: 4

This is an elegant side dish to serve with filet mignon or all by itself for a meal. Be sure to have a glass of champagne while you're fixing the sauce!

4 potatoes, baked and blossomed
4 oz. bacon, diced
1 onion, chopped
1 tbs. chopped shallot
½ cup chopped green bell pepper
4 oz. mushrooms, sliced
1 pkg. (10 oz.) frozen artichokes, thawed
1 cup *Demi Glace*, page 18
¼ cup champagne
1 tsp. Worcestershire sauce
1 tbs. finely minced parsley

In a large skillet, sauté bacon until it begins to brown. Add onion, shallot and green pepper and cook until softened. Stir in mushrooms and cook until tender. Add artichokes, *Demi Glace*, champagne and Worcestershire. Heat through. Divide evenly over prepared potatoes. Garnish with parsley.

CHICKEN AND ZUCCHINI

Servings: 4

We have a wonderful variety of fresh chicken readily available in today's grocery stores. Boneless chicken breasts, thighs, strips, cutlets and paillards make great timesavers in the kitchen. For variety, try adding mushrooms or sun-dried tomatoes to the sauce and serve it on spinach pasta.

4 potatoes, baked and blossomed
12 oz. fresh chicken
2 tbs. oil
2 tbs. butter
1 large onion
2 cloves garlic, minced

2 small zucchini, sliced
1 cup heavy cream
1 cup shredded Parmesan cheese, divided
salt and pepper to taste
1 tsp. freshly grated nutmeg

Cut chicken into ½-inch strips. Heat oil and butter in a large pan over medium high heat. Cut onion in half lengthwise and then into slivers. Sauté chicken until cooked through and beginning to brown. Remove and set aside. Add onion and garlic to pan and cook until soft. Add zucchini and cook until zucchini and onion are beginning to brown. Pour in cream. Return chicken to pan and sprinkle with half of the Parmesan. Cook, stirring constantly, until mixture begins to thicken. Season to taste with salt and pepper and add nutmeg. Divide evenly into prepared potatoes and sprinkle with remaining Parmesan.

CHICKEN BOURSIN

Servings: 4

This richly sauced potato is a meal in itself. Wine sauce is good on steak or burgers.

4 potatoes, baked and blossomed
1 tbs. butter
1 lb. fresh chicken breast, cut in strips
Red Wine Sauce, follows

8 oz. herbed cream cheese, such as
  Boursin, Rondele or Alouette, room
  temperature
1 tbs. finely minced parsley

In a skillet over medium high heat, melt butter and sauté chicken strips until opaque. Add *Red Wine Sauce*. Divide herbed cream cheese over prepared potatoes. Pour chicken and sauce over and garnish with parsley.

RED WINE SAUCE

3 tbs. butter
1/2 cup finely minced shallots
4 oz. mushrooms, finely minced
1 cup *Demi Glace*, page 18

1/4 cup robust red wine, such as
  burgundy
salt and pepper
pinch of cayenne

Melt butter in a large skillet over medium high heat. Sauté shallots until soft. Add mushrooms and cook until golden. Add *Demi Glace* and wine and bring to a boil, lower heat and simmer 5 minutes. Add seasonings to taste. Keep sauce warm while preparing chicken.

CHICKEN JERUSALEM

Servings: 4

We find that quartering mushrooms is more time-consuming but certainly more appealing visually. For a change of pace, substitute ¼ cup sun-dried tomatoes instead of the fresh tomato — delicious!

4 potatoes, baked and blossomed
¼ cup butter, divided
2 chicken breasts, skinned, boned and
  cubed
1 small onion, cut in slivers
1 cup sliced or quartered mushrooms
1 tomato, seeded and diced

1 cup artichoke quarters, frozen or
  canned in water
¼ cup sliced black olives
¼ cup brandy
¾ cup heavy cream
¼ cup grated Parmesan cheese

Melt 2 tbs. butter in a large skillet over medium high heat. Sauté chicken breasts until cooked through, stirring frequently. Remove and set aside. Melt remaining butter and cook onion until limp. Add mushrooms and sauté until tender. Add tomato, artichoke quarters, olives and chicken to skillet and heat through. In a small saucepan, heat brandy and ignite. Carefully pour into skillet. Stir until flames die down. Add cream and bring to a boil. Stir in cheese until melted. Divide evenly over prepared potatoes.

BISTRO CHICKEN

Servings: 4

Roasted red peppers in jars are one of our favorite pantry items. They add so much flavor to appetizers and main dishes — and opening a jar is certainly quicker than roasting them yourself.

4 potatoes, baked and blossomed
2 whole chicken breasts, skinned and boned
1 large onion
2 tbs. oil
3 cloves garlic, minced
1/2 cup roasted red peppers, cut in strips
1 cup sour cream
2 oz. proscuitto ham
salt and pepper to taste

Cut chicken breasts into 1/2-inch strips. Peel onion, cut in half lengthwise and cut into slivers. In a large skillet over medium high heat, cook chicken strips in oil until opaque. Remove and set aside. Add garlic and onion slivers and cook until golden brown. Stir in roasted peppers and sour cream. Return chicken to skillet and heat through. Season to taste with salt and pepper. Do not boil. Cut proscuitto into strips. Divide chicken mixture evenly over prepared potatoes. Garnish with proscuitto.

PORK MARSALA

This elegant entrée is easy to prepare when you use an off-the-shelf Demi Glace sauce (or you can prepare your own — see page 18). Look in the gourmet section of your grocery store, Knorr Swiss makes a nice one. In a pinch, you could use brown gravy mix. Cutting the onion into quarters and then into slivers as well as quartering the mushrooms, makes the presentation of this dish more elegant.

4 potatoes, baked and blossomed
1 lb. boneless pork strips
¼ cup butter, divided
1 clove garlic, minced
1 small onion, cut in slivers

1 cup mushrooms, quartered
¼ cup Marsala wine
1 cup prepared *Demi Glace* or brown
  gravy
salt and pepper to taste

Trim pork of fat and freeze for 30 minutes to facilitate slicing. Cut into bite-sized strips. In a large skillet over medium high heat, melt 2 tbs. butter. Stir-fry pork until cooked through, about 3 to 4 minutes, remove and set aside. Melt remaining butter in skillet and cook garlic until tender. Add onion and sauté until limp. Add mushrooms and cook until tender. Pour wine into pan and bring to a boil. Stir in *Demi Glace*. Taste and correct seasoning. Some mixes are quite salty and you'll only need a bit of pepper. Divide evenly over prepared potatoes.

POSH POTATOES

Leeks have a nice mellow flavor — a nice change of pace in this unusual topping.

4 potatoes, baked and blossomed
1 leek
¼ cup butter
1 cup sliced mushrooms
1 tsp. tarragon
2 tbs. flour
1 tbs. white wine
1 cup chicken broth
1 cup diced Brie cheese, rind removed
salt and white pepper to taste

Prepare leek by washing thoroughly. Trim off root ends and most of the green leaves. Cut leek into ½-inch rounds. Blanch, steam or microwave until tender. In a large skillet over medium high heat, melt butter. Sauté mushrooms until tender. Add prepared leek to skillet. Sprinkle with tarragon and flour. Stir in white wine and broth and bring to a gentle boil. Slowly stir in cheese until melted. Season to taste. Divide evenly over prepared potatoes.

POTATOES A LA RITZ

Servings: 4

*This elegant potato dish may turn up on **Lifestyles of the Rich and Famous**!*

4 potatoes, baked and blossomed
¼ cup butter
8 oz. filet mignon or other tender beef cut in strips
1 small onion, diced
½ cup sliced Shiitake mushrooms
½ cup sliced domestic mushrooms
½ tsp. thyme
salt and pepper to taste
1 cup sour cream

Melt 2 tbs. butter in a large skillet. Quickly sauté beef over high heat until done to your liking, 1 to 2 minutes for rare. Remove from skillet and set aside. Melt remaining butter and sauté onion until soft. Add mushrooms and cook until tender. Sprinkle with seasonings. Return meat to pan and add sour cream. Heat through but do not boil. Divide evenly over prepared potatoes.

PRIME POTATOES

Next time you go out for prime rib, order the biggest cut available and take the leftovers home in a doggie bag. This makes a sensational dinner the next day.

4 potatoes, baked and blossomed
1 cup sour cream
1 tbs. horseradish
2 tsp. Dijon mustard
1 tsp. salt
1 lb. prime rib, cut in strips
1 cup au jus, made from packaged mix, or beef broth
1 cup shredded cheddar cheese
2 green onions, thinly sliced

Combine sour cream, horseradish, mustard and salt in a small bowl. Heat meat strips in au jus until warmed through. Divide sour cream mixture evenly over prepared potatoes, top with meat, sprinkle with cheese and top with green onions.

BEEF WITH ARTICHOKES AND MUSHROOMS Servings: 4

An elegant topping — be sure to cook the filet until just rare to medium.

4 potatoes, baked and blossomed
1 lb. beef tenderloin filet
2 tbs. oil
2 tbs. butter
2 tbs. minced shallot or green onion
¼ lb. mushrooms

1 pkg. (10 oz.) frozen artichoke hearts, thawed
½ cup beef stock
½ cup cream
salt and pepper to taste
2 tbs. chopped parsley

Cut meat into 1-inch cubes. Heat oil in a heavy skillet until almost smoking. Cook beef quickly, turning with a spatula, until browned on all sides. Remove and set aside to keep warm. Add butter to skillet and sauté shallots until soft. Add mushrooms and cook until tender. Remove mushrooms from skillet and place in a bowl. Cook artichokes as directed on package, drain well and combine with mushroom mixture. Pour stock and cream into skillet and stir up any browned bits. Bring to a boil and cook rapidly to reduce mixture by half. Add vegetables and meat to sauce. Season to taste. Divide evenly over prepared potatoes and sprinkle with parsley.

VEAL PICCATA

Kitchen stores carry a terrific little tool called a "zester." It's wonderful for removing the zest (colored skin) of lemons, limes and oranges.

4 potatoes, baked and blossomed
3 tbs. flour
salt and pepper to taste
1 lb. veal scaloppine
2 tbs. olive oil
2 tbs. butter

1 clove garlic, minced
1 cup chicken stock
juice and zest of 1 lemon
1 tbs. capers
2 tbs. minced parsley

Place flour, salt and pepper in a plastic bag. Cut veal into strips. Dredge in bag and shake off excess. In a skillet over medium high heat, melt oil and butter. Quickly sauté veal until browned on both sides. Remove and set aside. In skillet drippings, cook garlic until soft, about 1 minute. Add chicken stock and cook until thickened, about 4 minutes. Add lemon zest, juice and capers. Return veal to pan and heat through. Divide evenly over prepared potatoes. Sprinkle with parsley.

VEAL WITH MUSHROOMS

Use a medium-bodied red wine such as Barbera, Bardolino, Valpolicella or Merlot.

4 potatoes, baked and blossomed
1 lb. veal for scaloppine
1 onion
1 cup shredded Fontina cheese
2 tbs. butter
2 tbs. olive oil
8 oz. fresh mushrooms, quartered
salt and pepper to taste

1 tsp. crumbled oregano
½ tsp. crumbled rosemary
½ cup red wine
1 cup *Demi Glace*, page 18 (or
    commercial variety)
2 tbs. minced parsley

Cut veal into 1-inch strips. Cut onion in half and then into slivers. Chill Fontina cheese for easier shredding. In a large skillet over high heat, melt butter with oil. Quickly sauté veal until cooked through. Remove and set aside. Turn heat to medium high. Sauté onion until limp. Add mushrooms and cook until tender and beginning to brown. Season with salt and pepper and sprinkle with oregano and rosemary. Add wine and *Demi Glace*. Return veal to skillet and heat through. Divide evenly into prepared potatoes. Sprinkle with cheese and parsley.

STUFFED POTATOES

CANLIS' STUFFED BAKED POTATO

Servings: 8

Canlis is one of Seattle's most famous and high quality restaurants. These potatoes are one of their specialties. We could make an entire meal out of these heavenly spuds!

4 potatoes, about 10 oz. each
¼ cup butter, room temperature
1 cup sour cream
salt and pepper to taste

1 tsp. white pepper
1 cup shredded Romano cheese
1 cup cooked, crumbled bacon
1 cup sliced green onions

TOPPING

¼ cup melted butter
½ cup shredded Romano cheese

1 tsp. paprika

Bake potatoes and cool to room temperature. Slice in half and scoop out centers into a bowl, leaving ¼-inch-thick shells. Place shells on a baking sheet. Whip centers with butter and sour cream until very smooth. Add salt and pepper to taste, and then white pepper. Fold in Romano cheese, bacon and green onions. Divide evenly into prepared shells. Cover and refrigerate if desired. To bake, heat oven to 400°. Drizzle tops of potatoes with melted butter and sprinkle with additional Romano and paprika.

IRISH MURPHYS

The Irish serve a potato dish with onion and cabbage, called Colcannon. This recipe is a variation of that theme and goes well with corned beef, baked salmon, or barbecued chicken.

4 potatoes, about 10 oz. each	2 tbs. butter
3 cups shredded cabbage	1 tsp. lemon juice
1 cup chopped onion	1/4 tsp. salt
1 tbs. oil	1/4 tsp. pepper
1/4 cup water	1/4 cup milk
1 tbs. soy	1 cup sour cream
1/2 tsp. dill	dill for garnish

Bake potatoes and cool to room temperature. Slice in half and scoop out centers into a bowl, leaving 1/4-inch-thick shells. Place shells on a baking sheet. In a medium saucepan, cook cabbage and onion in oil for 5 minutes. Add water, soy and dill; bring to a boil. Reduce heat, cover and simmer 10 minutes. Whip potato pulp with butter, lemon juice, salt and pepper. Stir in cabbage mixture and milk; whip until combined. Spoon into shells. Bake at 425° for 15 minutes or until heated through and tops are golden. Garnish with sour cream and sprinkle lightly with dill.

RED POTATOES WITH ROASTED GARLIC AND BLUE CHEESE

Servings: 4

Christie's father has a wonderful garden and grows delicious potatoes. We are fortunate to be able to get big fat red potatoes fresh from the garden — what a marvelous taste sensation when simply baked and served with butter. Try this recipe for a sensational accompaniment to simple roasts or barbecued meats.

1 large head garlic
4 large red potatoes, at least 10 oz. each
½ cup crumbled blue cheese

3 tbs. olive oil, divided
¾ tsp. salt
½ tsp. freshly ground black pepper

Cut ½ inch from the top of the head of garlic. Wrap garlic with foil and bake for 1 hour at 275° or until tender. Rub red potatoes with olive oil and bake until tender. Cool slightly and cut off tops. Remove potato pulp from potatoes, leaving a thin shell. Press garlic from skin and mash with a fork, add to potato pulp and mash well. Stir in blue cheese, salt, pepper and remaining olive oil. Spoon into potato shells. May be covered and refrigerated at this point. Place potatoes on a baking sheet and bake in a preheated 350° oven for 20 to 30 minutes.

CRAB AND CREAM CHEESE
STUFFED POTATOES

Servings: 8

A little crab goes a long way in this delicious and rich dish. Monterey Jack, cheddar or havarti would be good as well as the Swiss cheese.

4 potatoes, baked
4 oz. cream cheese, room temperature
2 tbs. butter
1 clove garlic, minced
2 green onions, sliced
1/2 cup mushrooms, sliced

8 oz. fresh crab
1 cup shredded Swiss cheese
salt and white pepper to taste
1/4 cup grated Parmesan cheese
2 tbs. chopped freshly parsley
1 tsp. paprika

Cut potatoes in half and scoop centers into a bowl, leaving a 1/4-inch shell. Place potato shells on a baking sheet. Add cream cheese to potato pulp and whip until light. In a small skillet, melt butter and sauté garlic until soft. Add green onions and mushrooms and cook until tender. Stir into potato mixture. Fold in crab and cheese and season with salt and white pepper. Spoon evenly into prepared shells, mounding in the center. Sprinkle with Parmesan, parsley and paprika. Bake in a preheated 350° oven for 20 to 30 minutes or until heated through and tops are golden.

SPINACH STUFFED POTATOES

Servings: 8

A perfect side dish for rack of lamb.

4 potatoes, baked
3 tbs. butter
3 tbs. milk
1 pkg. (10 oz.) frozen chopped, spinach, thawed
½ cup crumbled crisp bacon
2 green onions, thinly sliced
8 oz. Swiss cheese, shredded
salt and pepper to taste
1 tsp. paprika

Bake potatoes and cool to room temperature. Slice in half and scoop out centers into a bowl, leaving ¼-inch-thick shells. Place shells on a baking sheet. Using an electric mixer, whip centers with butter and milk until smooth. Place thawed spinach in a kitchen towel and wring tightly to remove excess moisture. Add spinach, bacon, green onions and cheese to the mixture and combine. Season to taste. Divide evenly into prepared shells. Sprinkle tops with paprika. Cover and refrigerate if desired. Bake in a preheated 400° oven for 20 to 30 minutes or until golden.

CHEESE AND CHILE STUFFED POTATOES

Servings: 8

These go well with barbecued salmon, steak or ribs and are a nice make-ahead for entertaining. Never use a food processor to whip potatoes, because it develops the gluten and turns them into a gluey mess.

4 potatoes, baked
3 tbs. butter
3 tbs. milk
1 can (4 oz.) can diced green chiles
8 oz. shredded cheddar
salt and white pepper to taste
1 tsp. paprika
sour cream and salsa for garnish

Let potatoes cool to room temperature. Slice in half and scoop out centers into a bowl, leaving ¼-inch-thick shells. Place shells on a baking sheet. Whip centers with butter and milk until smooth. Stir in chiles and cheddar; season with salt and pepper. Divide evenly into prepared shells and sprinkle tops with paprika. Cover and refrigerate if desired. Bake in a preheated 400° oven for 20 to 30 minutes or until golden. Serve with sour cream and salsa.

STUFFED YAMS WITH BACON AND DATES

Servings: 4

A different and tasty combination.

4 yams, baked until tender
8 slices bacon
¼ cup finely chopped green onion
¼ cup sour cream
2 tbs. brown sugar
2 tbs. butter, room temperature

1 egg yolk
½ tsp. salt
¼ tsp. nutmeg
½ cup finely chopped dates
sour cream for garnish

Bake yams at 375° for 45 minutes, or until tender. Cool and cut a thin slice off the top of each. Remove centers, leaving a ¼-inch shell. Place centers in a medium bowl. Cook bacon until crisp. Remove, drain on paper towels, cool and crumble. Mash centers well and add onion, sour cream, brown sugar, butter, egg yolk, salt, nutmeg, bacon and dates. Refill shells, mounding in center. Place in baking dish and bake at 400° for 20 minutes. Serve with sour cream.

MACADAMIA NUT STUFFED POTATOES

Servings: 8

A taste of Hawaii! If desired, sprinkle additional Swiss and chopped nuts on top.

4 potatoes, baked
¾ cup heavy cream
¾ cup chopped macadamia nuts
⅓ cup thinly sliced green onions
1 tsp. salt
½ tsp. white pepper
1 cup shredded Swiss cheese
2 tbs. shredded Swiss cheese for garnish
2 tbs. chopped macadamia nuts for garnish
1 tsp. paprika

Bake potatoes and cool slightly. Cut in half and remove centers, leaving a ¼-inch shell. Beat potato centers with cream until light; add remaining ingredients. Refill potatoes and place on a baking sheet. Bake at 350° for 15 minutes. Top with additional cheese and nuts and sprinkle with paprika. Bake until cheese melts and topping is bubbly.

SWEET POTATOES AND YAMS

TOPPINGS FOR SWEET POTATOES AND YAMS

In addition to the recipes we have included in this section, the following toppings go well with these tasty tubers.

- butter, brown sugar, diced canned peaches and cashews
- smoked chicken and apple sausage slices, chutney and toasted slivered almonds
- cooked pork sausage and applesauce
- thinly sliced green onions and shredded Jack cheese
- *Pineapple Salsa*, page 57
- cranberry chutney or relish
- butter, maple syrup and applesauce
- crumbled bacon, brown sugar and butter
- butter and orange marmalade

SWEET POTATO, HAM AND BOK CHOY SOUP

This light and tasty Chinese soup is great for weight watchers.

6 cups chicken broth
1 cup finely chopped ham
2 sweet potatoes, peeled and sliced
1 bunch bok choy
4 green onions, sliced
2 tsp. low sodium soy sauce
1 tsp. dark sesame oil

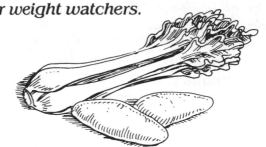

Heat chicken broth in a large saucepan over medium high heat. Stir in minced ham. Slice sweet potatoes into very thin slices using a food processor or by hand, and add to chicken broth. Remove leaves from bok choy and slice into 1-inch wide strips. Set aside. Slice stems of bok choy into l-inch slices on the diagonal and add to soup. Cook soup until sweet potatoes are tender-crisp. Add reserved leaves, green onions, soy and sesame oil to the soup. Cook just until leaves lose their crispness.

SCALLOPS ORIENTAL

Servings: 4

The apricot glaze in this sauce goes well with sweet potatoes or yams.

4 large sweet potatoes or yams, baked
  and blossomed
2 tbs. oil
1 lb. scallops
1 red bell pepper, cut in julienne strips
8 oz. snow peas, trimmed on the diagonal

1 can (8 oz.) sliced water chestnuts
4 green onions, cut into 1-inch lengths
  on the diagonal
Apricot Glaze, follows
1 tbs. chopped cilantro
1 tbs. toasted sesame seed

Heat oil in a large skillet over high heat, add scallops and stir-fry until semi-cooked. Remove and set aside. Add red pepper and snow peas and cook until tender-crisp. Add water chestnuts and green onions and heat through. Return scallops to skillet and add apricot glaze. Combine well and heat through. Divide evenly over prepared potatoes and sprinkle with cilantro and sesame seed.

APRICOT GLAZE

1 cup apricot jam
2 tbs. low sodium soy sauce

1 tbs. finely chopped fresh ginger
1/4 tsp. red pepper flakes

Combine sauce ingredients in a small bowl.

HOLIDAY SWEET POTATOES

Servings: 6-8

This is one of our favorite Thanksgiving recipes. It travels well, is easily doubled or even tripled, it's tasty, colorful and a cinch to make!

2 cans (18 oz. each) sweet potatoes or yams, drained
1 can (21 oz.) apple pie filling
1 can (18 oz.) whole cranberries
2 tbs. orange marmalade
2 tbs. apricot jam

In a colorful ovenproof casserole, approximately 8 inches square, place sweet potatoes, apple pie filling and whole cranberries; gently stir together. Combine marmalade and apricot jam and spread over top. Bake at 350° for 30 minutes or until bubbly.

SWEET POTATOES ANNA

Servings: 6

This dish is French in origin, where white fleshed potatoes are normally used. It can be assembled ahead and chilled before baking. Slicing the potatoes with the food processor makes preparation a breeze.

2 lb. sweet potatoes or yams, thinly
  sliced
½ cup butter, melted

6 tbs. grated Parmesan cheese
salt and white pepper to taste

Coat the bottom of a 9-inch cake pan with 1 tbs. of butter. Arrange ⅙ of the potatoes on bottom, drizzle with butter, sprinkle with 1 tbs. of cheese and season with salt and pepper. Continue layering in this fashion 5 more times. Cover with foil and press down with your hands to compress mixture. Chill overnight if desired.

To bake, heat oven to 425°. Place pan in oven and bake for 30 minutes. Uncover and continue baking for 40 to 45 minutes longer. Potatoes should be tender and top should be crisp and brown around edges. Remove from oven and let stand 5 minutes.

Using a large spatula to hold potatoes in pan, drain off excess butter. Loosen potatoes around the edges with a knife and invert onto a platter. With a sharp knife, cut into 6 wedges.

SWEET POTATOES WITH CASHEWS

Serves: 8

This makes a nice accompaniment to Cornish game hens or a Thanksgiving side dish.

2 cans (16 oz. each) sweet potatoes, drained
1 can (16 oz.) apricot halves
3 tbs. cornstarch
1/3 cup brown sugar
1 tsp. salt

1/3 cup sherry
2/3 cup golden raisins
2 tsp. grated orange zest
1/2 tsp. nutmeg
1 cup coarsely chopped cashews

Place sweet potatoes in a buttered ovenproof casserole. Drain apricots and pour liquid into a 2-cup measure. Add water to equal 2 cups. Add drained apricots to sweet potatoes. In a saucepan, combine cornstarch, brown sugar and salt. Add liquid and stir well. Bring to a boil over medium heat. Add sherry, raisins, orange zest and nutmeg. Cook, stirring constantly for 2 minutes. Pour over sweet potatoes and mix gently. Sprinkle with cashews. Cover with foil and bake at 350° for 30 minutes, remove foil and cook for 15 minutes longer.

SWEET POTATO MUFFINS

You can use yams or sweet potatoes in this recipe.

1 can (16 oz.) sweet potatoes or yams,
  drained
½ cup butter
1 cup sugar
2 eggs
1¼ cups milk
1 tsp. lemon extract
2½ cups flour

1½ tbs. baking powder
½ tsp. salt
1½ tsp. cinnamon
¾ tsp. nutmeg
1 cup golden raisins
¾ cup chopped pecans

Topping: ¼ cup sugar mixed with 1 tsp. cinnamon

Heat oven to 400°. Using an electric mixer, combine sweet potatoes, butter and sugar. Add eggs, milk and extract and mix well. By hand, stir in flour, baking powder, salt and spices. Add raisins and nuts; do not overmix. Prepare two 12-cup muffin pans by greasing well or lining with paper liners. Spoon batter evenly into cups and sprinkle with topping. Bake for 20 to 25 minutes or until center tests clean with a toothpick. Cool on a rack.

SWEET POTATO PIE

A tradition down South. Mash the sweet potatoes by hand so that the pie will have texture. If you like it sweeter, just add more sugar.

one 9-inch unbaked pie crust, chilled
4 medium sweet potatoes, baked and
  peeled
3 eggs, beaten
1½ cups half and half cream
¼ cup melted butter
⅓ cup sugar

1 tsp. cinnamon
½ tsp. nutmeg
½ tsp. allspice
½ tsp. salt
1 tsp. grated lemon rind

Heat oven to 400°. Mash sweet potatoes with a wooden spoon or potato masher. Using an electric mixer or food processor, combine eggs, cream, butter, sugar and spices. Stir into mashed sweet potatoes and pour into crust. Bake for 45 to 55 minutes or until set and a knife inserted in the center comes out clean. Cool completely before slicing. Serve at room temperature with sweetened whipped cream.

LOUISIANA SWEET POTATO PIE

Servings: 8

Sinfully rich, this sweet potato pie has a pecan topping. Next time you bake sweet potatoes, fix two or three extra and make this wonderful treat.

one 9-inch unbaked pie crust
1 cup baked sweet potato pulp
¼ cup brown sugar, packed
2 tbs. sugar
1 egg, beaten
1 tbs. butter
1 tbs. vanilla
¼ tsp. salt
½ tsp. cinnamon
⅛ tsp. allspice
⅛ tsp. nutmeg
Topping, follows

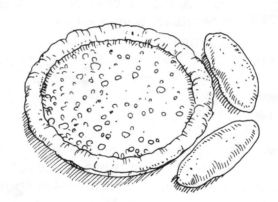

Heat oven to 325°. Combine sweet potatoes, sugars, egg, butter, vanilla, salt and spices until smooth. Pour into crust and pour topping over sweet potato mixture. Bake pie for 1½ hours, or until knife inserted in the center comes out clean. Cool and serve with whipped cream.

PECAN TOPPING

¾ cup dark corn syrup
¾ cup sugar
2 eggs
1½ tbs. melted butter
2 tsp. vanilla
pinch of salt
1 cup chopped pecans

Combine corn syrup, sugar, eggs, butter, vanilla and salt until smooth. Add pecans and stir gently.

BOURBON SWEET POTATOES

Servings: 8

Here is something special to add spice to your holiday buffet.

4 lb. yams or sweet potatoes
½ cup butter
½ cup bourbon
⅓ cup orange juice
grated zest of 1 orange
¼ cup brown sugar
1 tsp. salt
½ tsp. apple pie spice
½ cup chopped pecans

Cook and mash yams or sweet potatoes. Combine with butter, bourbon, orange juice, zest, sugar, salt and apple pie spice. Beat well. Place in a buttered 2-quart casserole dish and sprinkle with pecans. Bake at 350° for 45 minutes or until brown and bubbly.

GLAZED GRANNY SMITHS AND SWEETS

Servings: 8

The tart apples make a pleasant contrast to the sweet potatoes in this easy to assemble casserole.

¼ cup sugar
½ tsp. salt
¼ tsp. nutmeg
¼ cup butter
4 medium sweet potatoes, cooked and
  peeled

3 Granny Smith apples, cored and
  peeled
¼ cup hot water
⅔ cup brown sugar

Combine sugar, salt, nutmeg and butter in a small bowl. Thinly slice sweet potatoes and apples. Butter a 2-quart ovenproof casserole. Layer ⅓ of the sweet potatoes, ⅓ of the apples and sprinkle with ⅓ of the butter mixture. Repeat twice. Pour hot water over top, cover with foil and bake at 350° for 1 hour, or until apples are tender when tested with a fork. Remove from oven. Preheat broiler. Remove foil from top and press brown sugar through a wire mesh strainer evenly over top of casserole. Set under broiler until sugar melts and begins to bubble, about 2 to 3 minutes. Watch carefully so it does not burn.

SWEET POTATO AND PINEAPPLE PUFF

A bit of sherry instead of the vanilla is also good in this dish.

2 cans (16 oz.) sweet potatoes, well
 drained
½ cup butter, melted
2 eggs
1 cup sugar

1 tsp. pumpkin pie spice
1 tsp. vanilla or sherry
1 cup crushed, drained pineapple
1 cup golden raisins
Topping, follows

Using an electric mixer, combine potatoes, butter, eggs, sugar, spice and vanilla until fluffy. Stir in pineapple and raisins. Place in a buttered baking dish and sprinkle with topping. Bake at 325° for 30 minutes.

TOPPING

1 cup brown sugar
⅓ cup butter, melted
⅓ cup flour
1 cup chopped pecans

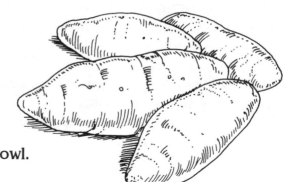

Combine topping ingredients in a small bowl.

SWEET POTATO SALAD
WITH CHUTNEY DRESSING

This is a most unusual salad. Add cubed ham, chicken or turkey for a main dish.

4 medium sweet potatoes
1½ cups diagonally sliced celery
1 cup well-drained pineapple chunks
1 cup red flame grapes
½ cup sliced green onions

½ tsp. salt
¼ cup orange juice
lettuce leaves, for serving
½ cup slivered almonds, toasted

Cook sweet potatoes in water to cover for 20 to 30 minutes or until just tender; do not overcook. Cool and cut into large cubes, making about 3 cups. Combine sweet potatoes, celery, pineapple, grapes, green onions, salt and orange juice in a large bowl. Add dressing and chill. To serve, place on lettuce leaves and garnish with toasted slivered almonds.

CHUTNEY DRESSING

l cup mayonnaise
2 tsp. curry powder

½ cup Major Grey's Chutney

Combine dressing ingredients. Thin with milk if necessary.

OTHER POTATO DISHES

LACY POTATO CUPS

Makes: 3 dozen

Teflon-lined miniature muffin tins are the greatest. We use them constantly for appetizers, small desserts and even muffins. Try this appetizer when you want to impress someone. We have included two delicious filling ideas. Years ago, Christi did some promotional appearances for a caviar company. She became quite an expert on the subject. Her personal favorite is American Golden Caviar. If you use an inexpensive brand, be sure to place it in a fine mesh sieve and rinse the caviar well under cold running water. Many of the less pricey brands are heavily dyed.

1 pkg. (24 oz.) frozen hash brown potatoes, thawed and squeezed dry
½ cup melted butter
salt to taste

Spray miniature muffin tins with nonstick cooking spray. Heat oven to 425°. Press a rounded tablespoon of shredded potatoes into each cup. Press firmly with your fingers with so that potatoes come over the top edge of the muffin tin. Bake for 10 minutes, brush with melted butter, sprinkle with salt and continue baking 10 to 15 minutes or until golden brown. Let cool in cups 2 minutes. Remove to paper towels to cool. May be made several hours in advance and kept at room temperature.

SOUR CREAM AND CAVIAR FILLING

1 pint sour cream
1 tiny jar (2 oz.) caviar, rinsed very well

Just before serving, fill each cup with a teaspoon of sour cream and a tiny dollop of caviar. Serve on a silver tray and decorate with lemons and parsley.

SHRIMP AND SALSA FILLING

1 pint sour cream
4 green onions, sliced
2 cups baby shrimp, divided
1 jalapeño, seeded and finely chopped
2 tbs. salsa
sprigs of cilantro

Combine sour cream, green onions, $2/3$ of the shrimp, jalapeño and salsa in a small bowl. Just before serving, fill each cup with a teaspoon of the sour cream mixture and garnish with a shrimp and a sprig of cilantro. Serve on a pottery tray and garnish with lime wedges and chile peppers.

CREAMY CHEESED POTATOES

Servings: 6

This recipe is unusual and tastes great with grilled steak or fish. A food processor makes preparation a snap. Tip: At the Cordon Bleu we learned that vegetables that grow underground are cooked covered and vegetables that are grown above the ground are cooked uncovered.

12 small red skinned new potatoes
2 tbs. butter
1 onion, chopped
4 green onions, thinly sliced
2 tbs. chopped parsley
1 tbs. chopped cilantro

½ tsp. oregano leaves
salt and pepper to taste
2 tomatoes, seeded and chopped
¾ cup cream
4 oz. mozzarella cheese, shredded

Scrub potatoes but do not peel. Place in a large pan and cover with water. Bring to a boil, reduce heat and cook gently for 20 minutes or until tender when pierced with a fork. Drain potatoes well and keep warm.

Melt butter in a large skillet over medium high heat. Add onion and cook until soft. Add green onions, parsley, cilantro, oregano, salt and pepper and cook for 1 minute, stirring. Add tomatoes, cream and cheese to skillet; stir until cheese is melted. Pour at once over hot potatoes and stir to combine.

CRISPY POTATO CASSEROLE

Servings: 6-8

Another quick way to dress up instant mashed potatoes. If made ahead, place the French fried onions on top just before baking.

2 cups mashed potatoes
8 oz. cream cheese, room temperature
1 small onion, finely chopped
2 eggs
2 tbs. flour
1 tsp. salt
½ tsp. white pepper
1 can (3½ oz.) can French fried onions, crumbled

Using an electric mixer, combine potatoes, cream cheese, onion, eggs, flour, salt and pepper until light and fluffy. Butter a 2-quart ovenproof casserole. Spoon potato mixture evenly into pan. Sprinkle onions evenly over top. Bake uncovered at 325° for 30 minutes.

RICH POTATO CASSEROLE

Servings: 6-8

You can also use frozen shredded hash browns for this recipe to save time.

9 medium potatoes, boiled, peeled, and shredded
1 can (10¾ oz.) cream of chicken soup
1 pint sour cream
1 tsp. seasoned salt
½ tsp. white pepper
½ cup green onions, thinly sliced
1½ cups shredded cheddar cheese
1 cup cornflake crumbs or crushed potato chips
¼ cup melted butter

Place potatoes in a large bowl. Combine soup, sour cream, salt and pepper. Stir into potatoes. Add onions and cheese and mix well. Pour into a greased casserole. Top with crumbs and drizzle with butter. Bake at 350° for 45 minutes or until potatoes are tender and top is brown and bubbly.

POTATO AND CARROT CASSEROLE

Servings: 12

A nice change from scalloped potatoes, this casserole has the tang of yogurt and the crunch of bacon and almonds. Try it with an Easter ham for a buffet.

6 medium potatoes, peeled and shredded
6 medium carrots, peeled and shredded
2 cloves garlic, minced
1 large onion, chopped
8 oz. sharp cheddar cheese, shredded
3 cups plain yogurt
1/3 cup salad oil

2 eggs, beaten
1 tsp. salt
1 tsp. seasoning salt
1 tsp. Worcestershire sauce
1/2 tsp. white pepper
1 cup sliced almonds
1 cup cooked, crumbled bacon

Combine potatoes, carrots, garlic, onion and cheese in a large bowl. Whisk together yogurt, oil, eggs and seasonings. Pour over vegetable mixture and combine well. Grease a 9-x-13-inch casserole or other baking dish. Top with almonds and bacon. Bake at 350° for 1½ hours.

POTATO CRUST QUICHE

Servings: 6-8

This is unusual brunch dish. You can vary the filling ingredients to suit your personal taste.

1 pkg. (24 oz.) frozen hash browns,
  thawed and squeezed dry
1/3 cup melted butter
1 cup shredded sharp cheddar cheese
1 cup shredded Swiss cheese

8 slices bacon, diced
1 large onion, chopped
2 eggs, beaten
1/2 cup half and half cream
1/2 tsp. seasoning salt

Press potatoes between paper towels to remove moisture. Place in the bottom and up sides of a 10-inch metal pie pan to form a crust. Brush with melted butter, especially top edges. Bake at 425° for 25 to 35 minutes until crisp and golden. While crust is baking, cook bacon in a skillet over medium high heat until crisp. Remove from pan, drain on paper towels and crumble. Reserve 2 tbs. bacon drippings. Sauté onion in drippings until golden. Beat eggs with cream and seasoning salt. Remove crust from oven and sprinkle with cheeses. Distribute bacon and onion on top of cheese and pour egg mixture over. Lower oven temperature to 350° and continue baking for 25 to 30 minutes or until eggs are set. Cut into wedges to serve.

POTATO AND ONION PIE

Servings: 8

The thin slicing blade of a food processor makes this recipe quick and easy.

4 lb. peeled potatoes, about 8 cups, thinly sliced
2 large onions, about 3 cups, thinly sliced
salt and pepper to taste
1/2 cup butter
1/2 cup shredded Parmesan cheese
cayenne pepper to taste

Preheat oven to 400°. In a buttered 9-x-13-inch baking pan, layer 1/3 of the potatoes with 1/3 of the onions, sprinkle with salt and pepper and dot with 1/3 of the butter. Repeat twice. Cover with foil and bake 45 minutes or until potatoes are tender when tested with a fork. Uncover and bake until top is golden, about 10 minutes. Remove from oven and cool in pan for 5 minutes. Loosen edges and invert on an ovenproof baking platter or rimmed cookie sheet. Sprinkle top with cheese and cayenne. Return to oven until cheese melts and top is crusty. Cut in squares to serve.

MUSHROOM AND POTATO PIE

Servings: 6

This can easily be made ahead or doubled for company. A bit of lemon juice added to the mushrooms helps keep the color from turning dark.

3 cups mashed potatoes (can use
  instant)
2 tbs. butter
½ cup finely chopped onion
1½ cups sliced fresh mushrooms

1 tsp. lemon juice
½ tsp. salt
pepper to taste
1 cup sour cream
paprika

Prepare potatoes and set aside. Melt butter in a large skillet over medium high heat. Sauté onion until limp. Add mushrooms, sprinkle with lemon juice and cook until soft. Sprinkle with salt and pepper. Butter a 9-inch pie pan or quiche pan. Place half of the potatoes in the pan and spread in an even layer. Top with mushroom mixture and spread with sour cream. Cover with remaining potatoes and sprinkle with paprika. May be refrigerated at this point. Bake at 350° for 35 to 45 minutes or until golden. Cut in wedges to serve.

SPICY POTATO PIE

Servings: 6

This is just the right accompaniment for roast beef or grilled steak.

3 cups mashed potatoes (can use instant)
1 tsp. salt
½ tsp. white pepper
1 tbs. hot horseradish
½ cup whipping cream, whipped until stiff
½ cup grated sharp cheddar cheese
paprika

Prepare mashed potatoes. Season to taste with salt, pepper and horseradish. Pour into a buttered ovenproof casserole or quiche pan. Top with whipped cream and sprinkle with cheddar and paprika. Bake at 350° for 25 to 30 minutes or until puffed and golden. Cut in wedges to serve.

QUICK RED POTATO SALAD

This is a great salad to take to potlucks.

3 lb. red potatoes
1 lb. bacon
1 bunch green onions, thinly sliced
2 cups ranch dressing
salt and pepper to taste

Boil potatoes in lightly salted water until tender. Drain and cool. Cut bacon into ½-inch pieces and fry until crisp. Remove from pan and drain on paper towels. Cut larger potatoes in halves or quarters. Combine all ingredients in a large bowl and season to taste. Cover and refrigerate for several hours to blend flavors. Stir well before serving and garnish with chopped parsley. If potatoes absorb too much dressing and mixture seems dry, add additional ranch dressing.

RED POTATO AND KIELBASA SALAD

Servings: 6

A hearty side dish. Look for one of the new lower fat kielbasas to cut calories.

1 lb. kielbasa sausage
1 tbs. oil
3 lb. red potatoes
¼ cup chicken stock
¼ cup white wine vinegar
2 tsp. salt

2 tbs. Dijon mustard
⅔ cup olive oil
¼ cup sliced green onions
¼ cup chopped parsley
freshly ground black pepper to taste

Cut sausage into ½-inch pieces on the diagonal. Heat oil in a large skillet and lightly sauté sausage until golden. Remove and set aside. Cook potatoes in boiling salted water until tender. Drain and transfer to a large bowl. Heat chicken stock and pour over potatoes. Let stand until absorbed. Cut any larger potatoes into halves or quarters. Combine vinegar, salt, mustard and olive oil in a food processor or blender. Pour over potatoes and stir to coat well. Add cooled sausage, green onions and parsley; season to taste with pepper.

GREEK POTATO SALAD

Servings: 6

To pit Greek olives, place a wide blade knife on top of the olive and pound it with your fist — presto, it's pitted.

4 cups torn Bibb lettuce
2 cups unpeeled red potatoes, cooked
  and sliced
2 cups cherry tomatoes, halved
1 cup sliced radishes

½ cup sliced green onions
¼ cup coarsely chopped parsley
½ cup crumbled feta cheese
1 cup pitted Greek olives

Arrange lettuce in bottom of a large salad bowl. Place potatoes, tomatoes, radishes, green onions, parsley and feta on the lettuce in a decorative fashion. Arrange olives around the edge. Just before serving, drizzle dressing over top and toss well.

DRESSING

¼ cup oil
2 tbs. red wine vinegar
1 clove garlic, minced

1 tsp. oregano leaves
½ tsp. salt
¼ tsp. freshly ground black pepper

Combine dressing ingredients in a food processor or blender.

GERMAN POTATO SALAD

An old-fashioned standby and family favorite. Sprinkle with additional parsley for color just before serving.

5 lb. red potatoes
1 lb. bacon, cut into quarters
1 large onion, diced
1/3 cup flour
1/2 cup water

1/2 cup cider vinegar
1 tbs. sugar
1/2 tsp. salt
pepper to taste
chopped parsley for garnish

Cook potatoes in salted water until tender, about 45 minutes. Drain and cool. Slice into an ovenproof dish. Fry bacon and remove from skillet. Reserve bacon fat. Sauté onion in 1 tbs. bacon fat until tender. Add onions and bacon to potatoes. Add flour to remaining bacon fat in skillet and mix well. Add water, vinegar, sugar, salt and pepper to skillet and cook until thickened. Pour over potato mixture and mix well. Bake at 350° for 45 minutes. Sprinkle with parsley and serve.

HEARTY BEEF AND RED POTATO SALAD

Servings: 6

This makes a complete meal on a hot summer night. Purchase roast beef at the deli and make the entire salad early in the day.

1 recipe *Vinaigrette*, follows
2 lb. small red potatoes
1½ lb. rare roast beef, cut into strips
½ red onion, cut into slivers
½ lb. mushrooms, quartered
1 small jar marinated artichoke hearts,
  drained

3 tomatoes, cut into wedges
3 tbs. crumbled blue cheese
2 tbs. chopped parsley
Bibb lettuce leaves for serving

Prepare *Vinaigrette* and divide in thirds. Marinate beef strips in one third and refrigerate for at least 3 hours. Cook potatoes in boiling water until just tender. Drain and cut any large potatoes into halves or quarters. Pour one third of the dressing over the warm potatoes, toss to coat, cover and refrigerate.

To assemble salad, line individual plates with lettuce leaves. In a large bowl, combine beef, potatoes, onion, mushrooms, artichokes and tomatoes. If necessary, add remaining dressing to moisten. Toss gently and divide evenly over plates. Sprinkle with blue cheese and parsley.

VINAIGRETTE

1 cup olive oil
1/2 cup red wine vinegar
1 clove garlic, minced
1 tbs. Dijon mustard
1 tsp. oregano flakes
1 tsp. salt
1 tsp. sugar
1/2 tsp. black pepper

Combine ingredients in a food processor or blender.

GRANDMA'S GREAT POTATO SALAD

Servings: 8

Everyone has their own "special" recipe for potato salad. This is our family's favorite. Add your own favorite ingredients to personalize it for your taste.

8 potatoes
6 eggs, hard cooked
1 cup mayonnaise
1 cup sour cream
2 tbs. Dijon mustard
1 tbs. rice wine vinegar
2 tsp. Lawry's seasoning salt
1 tsp. celery seed
3/4 cup chopped dill pickle
1/4 cup minced white onion

Boil potatoes until tender. Cool, peel, dice and place in a large bowl. Chop hard cooked eggs and add to potatoes. Combine mayonnaise, sour cream, mustard, vinegar, seasoning salt and celery seed. Gently fold into potato mixture. Stir in pickle and onion. Taste and correct seasoning as desired. Cover and chill for several hours before serving.

LITHUANIAN POTATOES

Servings: 6

This dish is so delicious, try to forget about the calories!

8 oz. bacon, diced
1 large onion, chopped
4 large potatoes, peeled and grated
4 eggs, beaten
1 cup milk
1 tbs. chopped parsley
salt and pepper to taste

In a large skillet, cook bacon until limp. Pour off excess fat and add onion. Continue cooking until bacon is crisp and onion is soft. Place potatoes in a large mixing bowl; add bacon mixture, eggs, milk and seasoning. Pour into a buttered baking dish. Heat oven to 375° and bake for 1 hour or until top is golden and potatoes are tender.

PUFFED POTATOES

Servings: 8

This is a different way to add flavor and interest to a potato topping. The peppers add color and the egg whites hold the mixture together. Serve this with meat loaf or roasted chicken.

4 potatoes, baked and halved
4 tbs. butter, melted
salt and pepper to taste
1/2 red bell pepper
1/2 yellow bell pepper

1/2 green bell pepper
1 tbs. olive oil
1 clove garlic, minced
2 egg whites, room temperature
1 cup grated Parmesan cheese

Place halved potatoes on a baking sheet. Drizzle cut surfaces with melted butter and sprinkle with salt and pepper. Cut peppers into julienne strips. Heat olive oil, add garlic and cook until soft. Add peppers and sauté until soft. Drain on paper towels and set aside to cool. Beat egg whites with an electric mixer until stiff. Fold in cheese and peppers. Divide evenly over tops of potatoes. Bake at 400° for 15 to 20 minutes or until piping hot and topping is puffed and golden.

POTATOES PEPERONATA

This Italian-style dish can be served hot as a side dish or at room temperature as a salad. It's colorful and goes well with grilled meat, sausage or chicken.

3 tbs. butter
1 tbs. olive oil
1½ lb. red potatoes, cooked until just tender
3 tbs. olive oil
1 cup thinly sliced onion
2 cloves garlic, minced
2 green bell peppers, cored, seeded and sliced into strips

2 red bell peppers, cored, seeded and sliced into strips
3 red tomatoes, seeded and diced
2 tbs. chopped parsley
1 tsp. salt
1 tsp. pepper
3 tbs. balsamic vinegar
¼ cup sliced green onions
2 tbs. chopped fresh basil leaves

Heat butter with olive oil in a large skillet. Cut potatoes into ½-inch slices and sauté until crisp and brown. Remove from skillet and set aside. Add 3 tbs. olive oil to skillet and sauté onion and garlic until limp. Add peppers and cook until tender. Stir in tomatoes and heat through. Add onion mixture to potatoes and season with parsley, salt, pepper and vinegar. Let stand several hours for flavors to develop. Just before serving, reheat if desired, or serve at room temperature. Garnish with green onions and basil.

POTATO PANCAKES

One of our favorite potato recipes ever! Serve with German-style sauerbraten or as a treat for breakfast.

6 medium potatoes, peeled and
   shredded
1 small onion, chopped
2 tbs. flour
2 eggs, beaten
1½ tsp. salt

½ tsp. pepper
2 tsp. freshly grated nutmeg
2 tbs. chopped parsley
½ cup crumbled crisp bacon, optional
1 cup butter

In a large mixing bowl, combine potatoes, onion, flour, eggs and seasonings. Add bacon if desired. Heat half of the butter in a large heavy skillet over medium heat. For each pancake, drop ⅓ cup potato mixture into hot skillet. Flatten with a spatula until ½-inch thick. When pancakes are golden on one side, turn and cook until crisp on the other, approximately 5 minutes total. Add more butter as necessary. Remove cooked pancakes to a platter lined with paper towels and keep warm in a low oven while frying remaining batter. If batter becomes too liquid, drain off some of the excess and discard.

COTTAGE POTATOES

A nice make-ahead dish to serve for company. Add the dill if you are serving this with fish.

1 cup sour cream
2 cups cottage cheese
1 clove garlic, minced
¼ cup onion, minced
2 tsp. seasoning salt
1 tsp. white pepper
1 tsp. dill weed, optional
6 medium potatoes, cooked, peeled and diced
1 cup shredded cheddar cheese
paprika

In a large mixing bowl, combine sour cream, cottage cheese, garlic, onion and seasonings. Fold in potatoes. Pour into a greased casserole. Bake at 350° for 45 minutes or until golden. Top with cheddar and sprinkle with paprika. Broil briefly to melt cheese.

SALMON HASH

Should you ever have any leftover salmon, this makes an unusual brunch entrée. Serve with poached eggs and fresh fruit.

2 potatoes, peeled and cut into ½-inch
  cubes
¼ cup butter
2 tbs. oil
1 clove garlic, minced
½ cup chopped onion
⅓ cup finely chopped celery

2 tbs. chopped pimiento
2 tbs. finely chopped green bell pepper
⅓ cup heavy cream
½ tsp. salt
½ tsp. white pepper
¼ cup minced parsley
1½ cups cooked flaked salmon

Cook potatoes in boiling salted water until just tender, about 5 minutes. Drain well and pat dry with paper towels. In a heavy skillet, melt 1 tbs. butter with 1 tbs. oil. Cook potatoes until crisp and golden. Remove and set aside. Melt 1 tbs. butter and 1 tbs. oil and sauté garlic, onion, celery, pimiento and green pepper until soft. Add to potatoes and stir in remaining ingredients. Press firmly into a shallow glass dish, cover and refrigerate for 24 hours. Melt 2 tbs. butter in a large skillet over medium high heat. Form salmon mixture into four patties, about ½-inch thick. Sauté until golden on both sides, about 5 minutes.

HAWAIIAN CORN CHOWDER

Servings: 8

The Portuguese population of Hawaii have brought their delicious linguisa sausage to the islands. If you don't care for the sausage, use ham, bacon or clams.

4 potatoes, peeled and diced
2 onions, chopped
1 cup chopped celery
4 cups chicken stock
1½ cups light cream
1 tsp. salt
½ tsp. white pepper
½ cup chopped parsley
1 tsp. dill weed
2 cups chopped Portuguese linguisa sausage
2 cans (17 oz. each) cream-style corn

In a large soup kettle, combine potatoes, onions, celery and chicken stock. Simmer until potatoes are tender. Add remaining ingredients and simmer until heated through.

GOLDEN AUTUMN SOUP

Servings: 8-10

This hearty soup is loaded with vegetables and makes a wonderful lunch for fall.

2 onions, chopped
2 stalks celery, chopped
½ cup butter
2 leeks, sliced
3 potatoes, peeled and chopped
3 carrots, sliced
3 cups chicken broth

1 can (16 oz.) pumpkin
1 tsp. salt
½ tsp. white pepper
1½ cups half and half cream
¼ cup green onion, sliced
¼ cup chopped parsley

Chop onions and celery. Melt butter in a large soup kettle. Sauté onion and celery until soft. Add remaining vegetables and cover with chicken broth. Cook until tender, about 30 minutes. Puree vegetables in a food processor or blender in batches. Return to kettle. Add pumpkin, salt and pepper. Simmer for 5 minutes. Add cream, heat through and adjust seasoning. Just before serving, sprinkle with green onion and parsley.

CURRIED POTATO AND ZUCCHINI SOUP

Servings: 4-8

A nice way to use an over-abundant zucchini crop. Soup can be made ahead and frozen. Add cream when reheating. Adjust curry to suit your taste.

4 large zucchini, with skin, chopped
2 onions, chopped
1 cup peeled, chopped potatoes
½ cup chopped parsley
4 cups chicken broth
½ to 1 tsp. curry powder
salt and white pepper to taste
½ cup cream
½ cup sour cream for garnish
chopped parsley for garnish

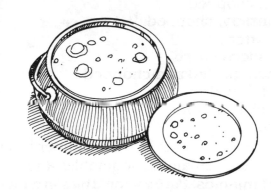

In a large soup kettle, combine zucchini, onions, potatoes, parsley and chicken broth. Simmer until tender. Season to taste with curry, salt and white pepper. Puree in batches in a food processor or blender. May be frozen at this point. To serve, reheat and stir in cream. May be served hot or cold, garnished with sour cream and chopped parsley.

SCALLOP CHOWDER

Servings: 6

This is one of the first recipes Christie made with a food processor in the mid-70s! It makes a nice winter supper served with sourdough bread and a green salad.

3 medium potatoes, peeled and sliced
1 large carrot, sliced
1 stalk celery, sliced
1 medium onion, chopped
2 cups chicken stock
½ tsp. thyme
1 bay leaf
1 tsp. salt

½ tsp. white pepper
2 tbs. butter
½ lb. fresh mushrooms, sliced
1 lb. fresh scallops
½ cup dry white wine
1 cup half and half cream
1 egg yolk, beaten

Place potatoes, carrot, celery and onion in a large soup kettle. Cover with chicken stock and add thyme, bay leaf, salt and pepper. Simmer over medium heat until vegetables are tender. Remove bay leaf. Puree mixture in food processor or blender in batches. Return to the pan but leave off the heat.

In a skillet, melt butter and sauté mushrooms until tender. Add scallops and wine and cook briefly until scallops are just turning opaque. Stir cream into egg yolk. Add scallop mixture and cream mixture to pureed vegetables. Heat through.

INDEX

SERVE CREATIVE, EASY, NUTRITIOUS MEALS WITH NITTY GRITTY® COOKBOOKS

Cappuccino/Espresso: The Book of Beverages
Worldwide Sourdoughs From Your Bread Machine
Indoor Grilling
Slow Cooking
The Best Pizza is Made at Home
The Well Dressed Potato
Convection Oven Cookery
The Steamer Cookbook
The Pasta Machine Cookbook
The Versatile Rice Cooker
The Dehydrator Cookbook
The Bread Machine Cookbook
The Bread Machine Cookbook II
The Bread Machine Cookbook III
The Bread Machine Cookbook IV
The Bread Machine Cookbook V

Recipes for the Pressure Cooker
The New Blender Book
The Sandwich Maker Cookbook
Waffles
The Coffee Book
The Juicer Book
The Juicer Book II
Bread Baking (traditional), revised
The Kid's Cookbook
No Salt, No Sugar, No Fat Cookbook, revised
Cooking for 1 or 2, revised
Quick and Easy Pasta Recipes, revised
15-Minute Meals for 1 or 2
The 9x13 Pan Cookbook
Extra-Special Crockery Pot Recipes

Chocolate Cherry Tortes and Other Lowfat Delights
Low Fat American Favorites
Now That's Italian!
Fabulous Fiber Cookery
Low Salt, Low Sugar, Low Fat Desserts
Healthy Cooking on the Run, revised
Healthy Snacks for Kids
Muffins, Nut Breads and More
The Wok
New Ways to Enjoy Chicken
Favorite Seafood Recipes
New International Fondue Cookbook
Favorite Cookie Recipes
Authentic Mexican Cooking
Fisherman's Wharf Cookbook

Write or call for our free catalog.
BRISTOL PUBLISHING ENTERPRISES, INC.
P.O. Box 1737, San Leandro, CA 94577
(800) 346-4889; in California (510) 895-4461